PHILOSOPHY AND CURRICULUM

ENCYCLOPAEDIA OF SCHOOL CURRICULUM

Vol. IV

PHILOSOPHY AND CURRICULUM

By

Prof. Marlow Ediger
M.A., B.S.E., Ed.D.
Emeritus Professor of Education
Truman State University
201 West 22nd Street
North Newton KS 67117
United States of America

&

Prof. Digumarti Bhaskara Rao
M.Sc., M.A., M.A., M.Ed., Ph.D.
Principal
R.V.R. College of Education
D-43 (277) S.V.N. Colony
Guntur - 522 006 (India)

DISCOVERY PUBLISHING HOUSE PVT. LTD.
NEW DELHI-110 002

ISBN: 978-81-7141-631-8

Philosophy and Curriculum

Published by:
DISCOVERY PUBLISHING HOUSE PVT. LTD.
4383/4B, Ansari Road, Darya Ganj
New Delhi-110 002 (India)
Phone: +91-11-23279245; 23253475; 43596065
+91 9811179893 / +91 9871656464
E-mail: discoverybooksindia@gmail.com
orderdphbooks@gmail.com
namitwasan9@gmail.com
web: www.discoverypublishinggroup.com

Printed at:
Infinity Imaging Systems
Delhi

Preface

Philosophy and Education are the two sides of the same coin. As one of the major areas of educational enterprise, the curriculum is influenced by Philosophy to a large extent. Considering the inter-relationship between Philosophy and Curriculum, this book on "Philosophy and Curriculum" is written to provide preservice and inservice teachers an opportunity to study and appraise diverse schools of thought in determining objectives, learning activities, and evaluation procedures for pupils. We tried to make the content as practical and utilitarian as possible for teachers. We believe strongly that educators and teachers need to possess a strong framework from which the curriculum for pupils may be envisioned and brought forth. Philosophy is a practical subject which has its many applications in curriculum development. We hope the curriculum designers will use the ideas from this book in developing the best curriculum possible for pupils.

Marlow Ediger
Digumarti Bhaskara Rao

CONTENTS

CONTENTS

1

Philosophy in the Educational Arena

Educators need to be well-versed in the philosophy of education and how it effects decisions made in the school curriculum. Standards guide the decision-making arena. These guidelines assist in following one path of teaching compared to other paths. Teachers, supervisors, and administrators disagree, in degrees, pertaining to deeds and acts to pursue in education. Philosophical differences are then in evidence.

Individuals differ from each other in many ways. Not only are there differences in interests, achievements, beliefs, and motivation in evidence, but also how to attain goals in life. Each goal itself might well emphasize divergent thinking pertaining to philosophical beliefs. To know if goals have been attained, philosophical approaches in appraising also appear. Each choice made in the societal arena stresses a point of view or a philosophy.

Educators used to be aware of how one's philosophy affects selection of goals, activities and experiences to achieve each goal, as well as means of evaluation to ascertain if goal attainment is in evidence.

There are numerous ways of dividing the world of objectives, activities and experiences, as well as evaluation procedures. Pertaining to a need for philosophy of education, Ozmon and Craver[1] wrote:

A study of philosophy of education seems imperative today for we are in a critical era of transition. There has always been change, but seldom at our present accelerated rate, creating in many individuals what Alvin Toffler has called the sickness of "future shock." In such an age, it is easy for people either to embrace more and more with little thought to eventual consequences or to resist change with little or no matter what. Educational philosophers, regardless of the particular theory they embrace, suggest that the solutions to our problems can best be achieved through critical and reflective thought.

In one basic sense, we can say that philosophy of education is the application of philosophical ideas to educational problems. We can also say with equal force that the practice of education leads to a refinement of philosophical ideas. From this viewpoint, educational philosophy is not only a way of looking at ideas but also learning how to use them in the best way. No intelligent philosophy of education is involved when educators do things simply because they were done in the past. A philosophy of education becomes significant at the point where educators recognize the need to think clearly about what they are doing and to see what they are doing in the larger context of individual and social development.

Realism as a Philosophy of Education

Realism emphasized a world, in existence, independent of observes. The objective world, natural and social phenomena, exists and is. The real world is not dependent upon any observer being present. The independent world can be known in whole or in part as it really is. Thus, any observer may receive a replica of the natural and social environment; rather than receive ideas only, from these phenomena.

Accuracy in describing the real world is a must. Numerically, this can be done. The independent universe might then be described with the use of numbers. Accurate description is possible with assigned numbers. The amount of each element and compound present can be described numerically. Mind being like a blank sheet at birth receives subject matter directly from reality.

Philosophy in realism becomes scientific. The methods of science are important to the realist. Objectivity is a key concept of realism in securing subject matter knowledge. Subjective ideas have no place in the scheme of things, according to realists. The scientist desires to describe reality as it really is. Emotions and feelings are left out. A true statement is one that corresponds with objects, items, and matter being described. Factual information, not opinions, are desired. Reality is not created, but may need to be changed as new discoveries are made.

In emphasizing science and philosophy as being one and not separate entities, Bertrand Russell[2] wrote:

> The first characteristic of the new philosophy is that it abandons the claim to a special philosophic method or a peculiar brand of knowledge to be obtained by its means. It regards philosophy as essentially one science, differing from the special sciences merely by the generality of its problems, and by the fact that it is concerned with the formation of hypothesis where empirical evidence is still lacking. It conceives that all knowledge is scientific knowledge, to be ascertained and proved by the methods of science. It does not aim, as previous philosophy has usually done, at statements about the universe as a whole, nor at the construction of a comprehensive system. It aims only at clarifying the fundamental ideas of the sciences, and synthesizing the different sciences into a single comprehensive view of that fragment of the world that science has succeeded in exploring.

Russell believed the world of science to contain that which is precise, measurable, and objective. Atomic and molecular statements were analysed by Bertrand Russell. Atomic statements correspond one to one with reality. Thus four plus five equals nine can be compared directly to the real world with four objects joined to five objects resulting in nine objects. Molecular statements contain two or more atomic statements. Breaking down the molecular statement into component parts makes possible atomic statements. Russell's brand of realism is called logical positivism. He accepted science (use of senses and empiricism) and mathematics (logical reasoning emphasizing specific accurate ideas) as the only two sources of knowledge. All other fields of knowledge represented opinions rather than objective statements. Logical positivists believe that language is so often misused making for a lack of clear communication. The business of science is to communicate clearly with one to one correspondence between each word and what it represents in the environment. The test of truth here is the correspondence theory. Truth is that which in a statement relates directly to what is present in the real, objective world. It is then possible to verify if a statement is true. Agreement by observes in science makes the statement true or false. Methods of science are needed to test data to determine what is true. Empirical methods of testing accept what is true and modify or rufute other statements as being false.

Realists emphasize the importance of the certainty of knowledge as compared to that which is dogmatic, opinion, and expresses emotions. Knowledge that is certain can be tested and verified. Only what can be verified and is true should be accepted. Knowledge needs to be discovered with the use of scientific methods and attitudes. Tradition and customs do not suffice as knowledge.

Realists believe there is nothing beyond scientific knowledge. Knowledge can be obtained from the use of the senses and nature.. Supernaturalism does not exist since it attempts to go beyond sense data. Matter in the universe then represents ultimate reality. Knowledge is not made by human beings. What exists in nature and in matter is independent of the observer and can be known in its entirety or in part. Then the universe can go and operate without human beings. Biases, prejudices, and emotions need to left out when individuals study the real world in an objective manner. The observer needs to discover and learn about nature and matter as it truly is, not as he/she would want it to be.

The realist desires objectivity and exactness in knowledge, not relative content nor human made ideas.

The realist educator emphasizes precision in stated objectives for teaching and learning situations. Either a learner achieves or does not attain any one objective. Learning opportunities need to be selected which aid students to attain objectives. No other activities and experiences in the curriculum are necessary or needed.

Idealism as a Philosophy of Education

Idealism emphasizes the world of ideas about the natural and social environment as being salient. It does not stress knowing objective reality as it truly exists and is. One can only receive ideas about what is seen, felt, tasted, touched, and smelled. Mind is real and needs to be developed. Mind is the most important part of the person science it develops ideas. Ideas become of major significance rather than the external world which is not knowable in and of itself. To develop quality ideas, the mind needs to experience that which is challenging and motivating. An alert mind is desired to secure vital ideas from the physical and social environment.

Mental development is then of utmost importance. What exists can only be known through ideas acquired. The mind or mental facet needs the best education possible. The mental, interprets the physical, not the physical interpreting the mental. The world of ideas becomes paramount.

Universals rather than particulars about the natural/social environment need acquisition. The general is to be preferred above the specific. Universals, such as generalizations and concepts, represent broad ideas covering many specifics. Specifics such as facts might well support a generalization or a concept. The mind develops universals (ideas) about the environment.

Generalizations (broad ideas) and concepts (covering many precise items) may pertain to such items in the abstract as trees, forests, cities, plains, plateaus, democracy, and socialism, among others. Pertaining to each of these items, abstractions are developed in terms of ideas. The will (effort) of the person must be involved to obtain the abstract to develop generalizations and concepts. Interest alone is not adequate to achieve, grow, and develop. To attain, the person must will to do so. To make progress might well mean hurdling the unpleasant.

Idealism has a longer history than do other philosophies of education. The human mind tends to develop ideals. These ideals emphasize goals to strive toward. Diverse organizations in society have objectives to achieve. The mind formulates these objectives or ideas be it within a club, an organization, the family, the religious group, or a governmental system.

Philosophers are concerned with *what* is ultimately real. Realists believe that what is observed, felt, tasted, heard, and smelled represents ultimate reality. Thus scientific experiments, carefully controlled, provide what is real and independent of the observer. No biases and prejudices are wanted in the outcomes of these experiments. The idealist, of course, accepts science as a way of securing information. However, the idealist believes that science and the scientific method are too limiting to determine what is ultimately true. Idealism stresses that truth comes from something beyond the world of sense data.

Ultimate reality, according to idealists, comes from the use of reason. The reasoning person develops ideas which transcend sense data in a science laboratory. Thus beyond that world of sense data and everyday experiences are ideas or purposes. Life consists of purposes in whatever each human being is to do. The purposes are to achieve ideas. Humans have long held ideas and ideals such as truth, justice, beauty, and honour in high esteem. Each person's purpose in the here and now is to achieve these ideals.

Beyond the here and now is God, for many idealists. It takes more than one lifetime to achieve vital ideas, be it in the here and now, as well as the hereafter. This life then may well not be the finality of one's deeds and acts. The here and now might be a testing ground for the hereafter, also called heaven. Thus beyond sense perception, many vital happenings transpire.

Human beings are at the top of living things. They are much higher in significance and importance, as compared to what is called animal life. Each person has a mind, an intellect, and a soul. The mind, intellect, or soul unite the person with Eternity and the life to come. The physical part of the person at death separates itself from the spiritual. The spiritual is not matter, but emphasizes that which is important about the person, such as the soul. The soul, mind, and intellect may be conceived as a unity, not as separate entities. Human beings, finite or limited in nature, desire to be a part of the Infinite or God.

The Infinite is the same yesterday, today, and forever. The planet earth may have its many changes in nature and society. However, the Infinite represents the changeless eternal. The person's ideas of Truth may change rather continuously, but the Infinite does not change and represents perfection.

Eternal values such as truth, beauty, goodness, and justice exist and have always existed. Thus, each person needs to discover these vital concepts. The mind, properly cultivated and educated, may discover these Truths though reason and thought. Rational thinking is then involved. Reasoning might well be the way to discover truth beauty, goodness, and justice.

Idealism emphasizes the coherence theory in testing statements to evaluate truthfulness. Thus a statement is true if it fits in logically with other statements. It is false if one experiences an illogical situation in attempting to fit in a new statement with others accepted as being true by idealists. Reason is utilized to determine if the new relates directly to other ideas previously accepted as being true. The mind and reason here are useful tools to accept or refute new subject matter. Pertaining to idealism, Brubacher[3] wrote:

> The most prolific writer on the idealistic philosophy of education in the Twentieth century was Herman Harrell Horne (1874-1946). At a time when idealism was already fast fading as the dominant American theory of education, Horne managed to draw together the various strains of idealism into their more systematic educational exposition. In addition to much that is already familiar he made two points of his own. One is his emphasis on volition and effort in learning. The pupil is like the plant, he agreed with Froebel, in that his response is self-active. But the child is unlike a plant, Horne continued, in that he can withhold his response. Hence the ultimate responsibility for getting an education rests on the will of the pupil. All education, therefore, is self-education; it is the result of voluntary effort put forth by a self-active mind. If effort is aided and abetted by interest, well and good. If not, then like Kant, Horne urged that the pupil in any case put forth effort in obedience to what he ought to do.
>
> A second and perhaps more notable point in Horne's exposition is the fact that he did not make any significant alteration in the developmental theory of education in the light of the Darwinian theory of evolution, which was introduced to the world after the deaths of Hegel and Froebel. To be sure, Horne saw that evolution had made the developmental process irreversible and unrepeatable, in contrast to the Aristotelian pattern of matter endlessly reproducing the cycle of changes demanded by its form. The Absolute, however, had no difficulty in assimilating this new theory of development, for Horne could still say that the Absolute

is; only the finite becomes. Pedagogically speaking, this seems to mean that through education the child still becomes in time what he was eternally meant to be.

Experimentalism as a Philosophy of Education

Experimentalists believe that one *experiences* the natural/ social environment. One cannot know the natural/social environment as it truly is, as the realist indicates. Nor does one receive ideas only, as the idealist believes. The individual interacts with the environment and thus experiences reality. Experiences then are the raw materials of life. One can only know that which is experienced.

Along with experiences, change abounds. Accelerated changes certainly are in evidence. Inventions, technology, and creativity in unique ideas bring on change within the world of experiences. Problems arise with changing situations. Problem solving becomes vital when viewing changing scenes and situations. Each problem needs careful identification with inherent clarity of content. Subject matter needs securing, directly related to each problem. The content or possible answers to the identified problem should be plausible and logical resulting in a hypothesis. A hypothesis is tentative and subject to testing within a contextual situation. Reference materials (concrete, semi-concrete, and the abstract) are data sources to test each hypothesis. If evidence warrants, the hypothesis is refuted or modified. Problem solving approaches are major methods to utilize in the curriculum.

Experimentalists advocate integrating school and society. School and society should definitely not be separated entities. Rather, within the curriculum, problems are identified and solved that have subject matter emphasizing societal concerns. What is relevant in the societal arena is salient for students in terms of problems to identify or solve. The oneness of school and society is important in experimentalism. Other dualisms are also frowned upon by experimentalists. Content and method are one, not discrete items. Thus content is acquired by students to solve problems in which problem solving is the method of instruction. The student individually and the societal arena of groups and committees should not be separated. Each individual interacts with others in school and in society. Thus, committee endeavours to solve problems in the school curriculum harmonize the concepts of the individual with society.

Experimentalists are strong proponents of having input from all who are to be affected by a decision made. Group/ committee endeavours should then be in evidence in decision making. No one should be left out of decision-making if the results are in effect. The individual interests with others in society and thus needs to have input into choices, decisions, ideas, and alternatives.

Experimentalists are strong in noticing the consequences of an act. The results of an act or deed need to be observed. Modification and change of the act or deed may then be necessary. Idealists tend to look at the intent of the person in the making of choices, rather than the consequences. For idealists, the Golden Rule has always been an ideal. Prior to its implementation, the Golden Rule had always been important. The Golden Rule then is in evidence prior to experience by anyone. Prior to experience is known as *a prior* statements. Experimentalists, however, emphasize the *a posteriori*. A posteriori looks to experience and its consequences for that which works.

Experimentalists believe in an inductive procedure of securing information to solve problems. Thus, from the specific to the general is emphasized. Specific subject matter is acquired to arrive at solutions to a problem. From each specific item, a generalization is attained in answer to the selected dilemma situation.

Reconstructionist philosophy is directly related to experimentalism. Reconstructionists believe that needed changes are urgent to make in the societal arena. Being neutral in dilemma situations has little or no value. One needs to study society and identify evils as problems to be solved. Information is developed into a hypothesis. The hypothesis is tested and revised, if needed.

Society provides a learning laboratory from which problems are identified. Society needs to be reconstructed based on problems selected from the societal arena. Street people, poverty, drug abuse, crime ridden areas, violence, murders, and racial discrimination represent what exists in society. These are problems evident in society. Each problem needs solutions. New problems arise as society changes. Urgency is involved in identification and solution to problems.

Reconstructionism emphasizes redoing society due to the many changes which must be made. Pertaining to experimentalism, Atkinson and Maleska[4] wrote:

> To a follower of Dewey, education has two sides—psychological and social; neither may be subordinated or neglected. The psychological nature of a child forms the basis for his education—it is the teacher's responsibility to make full use of his natural, spontaneous activities. Describing original nature as being spontaneously impulsive rather than passive, Dewey divided impulses into four kinds: the social impulses of communication or conversation; the constructive impulses to make things; the impulse to investigate things; and the impulse of artistic or creative expression.
>
> With these impulses in mind, said Dewey, the school must be changed from a place for sedentary listening to one for active doing or working. The teaching process must be planned to allow the child to learn wherever possible by his own experiences and, in that way, to acquire the habit of thinking. A proper solution to any problem demands intelligent thinking, which becomes the principle factor in the ability to cope with new situations. Thinking, as Dewey defined it, is the use of the meanings of past experiences in the interpretation of new situations.
>
> Dewey felt that when the psychological and social approaches to learning are separated. There is produced either a forced and external education in which freedom of the individual is subordinated to a preconceived notion of what society should be, or else a barren and formal development of the mental powers in which the learner has little idea of the use to be made of what is being learned. The school is primarily a social institution because its processes are social—in fact, educational processes are basically no different from those going on continuously in life outside the classroom.
>
> Therefore, Dewey claimed, the manner in which pre-school learning has been taking place should suggest to a teacher the logical starting point for more systematic encouragement of physical and mental growth. The school ideally should be that

form of social life into which can be concentrated those factors that most effectively cause a child to share the accumulated knowledge and skills of the race. Education can be considered as proceeding most satisfactorily whenever the individual is actively participating in social relationships with others.

Existentialism as a Philosophy of Education

Existentialists believe that first one exists, then finds his/her essence in life. Existentialism takes the opposite philosophy of Rene Decartes (1596-1650) who stated "I think therefore I am." Thus, an existentialist first is a being and then develops his/her own goals, purposes, interests, and values in life. Jean Paul Sartre (1904-1980), as an atheistic existentialist, believed in complete freedom for human beings to develop into the kind of person desired. With no God, Sartre emphasized that a supernatural being did not exist who could manipulate individuals on the planet earth.

With freedom in its entirety, the person can make many, many choices and decisions in context. The individual alone governs the kinds and types of choices made. No other person can then shoulder responsibilities for personal deeds and acts.

Existentialists believe in the absurdity of life. Life is not rational nor objective. The irrational and the subjective are vital facets of every day situations.

Choices and decisions made can be awesome. They might result in fear, alienation, and tremendous anxiety. However, to be human means to make choices and decisions. One can delegate to others the making of selections, from among many, but this is a personal decision. Human elements are lacking if the choices and decisions are delegated to others. In everyday life, individuals make selections with involved anxiety. Sartre emphasized that "man is condemned to be free". Many responsibilities then become an inherent part of the individual's life. In his essay "Man is Freedom", Sartre[5] wrote:

> It is strange that philosophers have been able to argue endlessly about determinism and free will, to cite examples in favour of one or the other thesis without ever attempting first to make explicit the structures contained in the very idea of action. The

concept of an act contains, in fact, numerous subordinated notions which we shall have to organize and arrange in a hierarchy; it is to produce an organized instrumental complex such that by a series of concatenations and connections the modification effected on one of the links causes modifications throughout the whole series and finally produces an anticipated result. But this is not what is important for us here. We should observe first that an action is on principle intentional. The careless smoker who has through negligence caused the explosion of a powder magazine has not acted. On the other hand the worker who is charged with dynamiting a quarry and who obeys the given orders has acted when he has produced the expected explosion; he knew what he was doing or, if you prefer, he intentionally realized a conscious project.

This does not mean, of course, that one must foresee all the consequences of his act. The emperor Constantine, when he established himself at Byzantium, did not foresee that he would create a center of Greek culture and language, the appearance of which would ultimately provoke a schism in the Christian church and which would contribute to weakening of the Roman Empire.. Yet he performed an act just in so far as he realized his project of creating a new residence for emperors in the Orient. Equating the result with the intention is here sufficient for us to be able to speak of action. But if this is the case, we establish that the actions necessarily implies as its condition the recognition of a "desideratum"; that is, of an objective lack or again of a negetite. The intention of providing a rival for Rome can come to Constantine only through the apprehension of an objective lack: Rome lacks a counterweight; to this still profoundly Pagan city ought to be opposed a Christian city which at the moment is missing. Creating Constantinople is understood as an act only if first the conception of a new city has preceded the action itself or at least if this conception serves as an organizing theme for all later steps. But this conception can not be the pure representation of the city as possible. It apprehends the city in its essential characteristic, which is to be a desirable and not yet realized possible.

Perennialism as Philosophy of Education

A prescribed curriculum is in evidence according to advocates of perennialism. The prescribed objectives, learning opportunities, as well as appraisal procedures, consist of enduring ideas which have stood the test of time and place. To endure, subject matter has to age and not be culled or forgotten. Recently written content might not survive in importance. Thus, time is needed to determine if ideas will become great, salient, and vital.

Classical content has a reputation to present the greatest ideas ever produced and can be called the Great Books, as a concept. The Great Books might then provide general education for all students. General education, not vocational education, may provide common learnings for these learners. If all students have access to the Great Books, common facts, concepts, and generalizations will be available to learners, students may then communicate a core of ideas with others. Specialized education in training for a job, vocation, or profession should come after the baccalaureate degree years. Mulhern wrote the following:

> While, no doubt, his demand that the problems of modern society be taught realistically alarmed social conservatives, his caustic criticism of traditional education in all its basic aspects become a matter of widespread questioning. Here was a social reformer who carried his respect for individuality to a point viewed by many as dangerous. To have stressed "change" and have rejected the "enternal varieties" as Dewey did, appeared to some of his critics to be an unsound approach to education. Leading the attack upon what they deemed Dewey's anti-intellectualism and his brand of naturalism were Robert M. Hutchins and Mortimer J. Alder who, followers of Aristotle's naturalism and his doctrine of the uniformity of nature, hold that there are natural truths that do not change and that such truths should be made the fixed intellectual content of education. Since human nature and truth, they hold, are everywhere the same, education and its basic aims should be always and everywhere the same. Dewey agrees that human nature is everywhere the same but argues that the mode of satisfying its needs differs in different environments, and that environmental conditions, rather than human nature, should be the guiding factor in education. And he rejected all "absolutes" and all doctrines of unchanging "truth".

Summary

Each philosophy has a school of thought to provide guidance and direction to teachers, and other workers in the school environment.

Realism places its emphasis upon objectivity of subject matter with science and mathematics presenting models to teachers in the classroom setting.

Idealism with its idea centered curriculum places emphasis upon literature and history as models in the curriculum. The learner is to move away from the finite and in the direction of the Infinite (God). Abstract subject matter needs acquisition by students in an idea centered curriculum to nourish the mind, soul, and spirit.

Experimentalism emphasizes the world of experience with its inherent changes. Flexible steps are needed to solve problems in a world of change.

Existentialism faces problems of human existence. Each person makes or breaks the self through the making of choices in an absurd world.

Perennialists reflect conservatism of ideas and look to the past for subject matter in the curriculum. Those ideas from the Great Books, enduring in time and place, need emphasis in teaching-learning situations.

Hopkins[6] Wrote:

> Philosophy has entered into every important decision that has ever been made about curriculum and teaching in the past and will continue to be the basis of every important decision in the future... . When a state office of education suggests a pupil-teacher time schedule, this is based upon philosophy, either hidden or consciously formulated. When a course of a study is prepared in advance in a school system by a selected group of teachers, this represents philosophy because a course of action was selected from many choices involving different values. When high school teachers assign to pupils more homework for an evening than any one of them could possibly do statisfactorily in six hours, they are acting on philosophy although they are certainly not aware of its effect. When a teacher in an elementary school tells a child to put away his geography and study his arithmetic she is acting on philosophy for she has made a choice of values. If she allowed the child to make the choice she would have been operating under a different set of beliefs... . When teachers shift subject matter from one grade to another, they act on philosophy. When measurement experts interpret their test

results to a group of teachers, they act upon philosophy, for the facts have meaning only within some basic assumptions. There is rarely a moment in a school day when a teacher is not confronted with occasions where philosophy is a vital part of action. An inventory of situations where philosophy was not used in curriculum and teaching would lead to a pile of chaff thrown out of educative experiences.

REFERENCES

1. Ozman, Howard, and Craver, Samuel. *Philosophical Foundations of Education*. Columbus, Ohio: Merrill Publishing Company, 1990, p. XII.
2. Wahlquist, John T. *The Philosophy of American Education*. New York: The Ronald Press, 1942, pp. 60-61.
3. Brubacher, John S., *A History of the Problems of Education*. New York: McGraw-Hill Book Company, 1996, pp. 128 and 129.
4. Atkinson, Carroll, and Maleska, Eugene T. *The Story of Education* New York: Chilton Books, 1965, pp. 87 and 88.
5. Tillman, Franklin A., Berofsky, Bernard., and O'Conner, John. *Introductory Philosophy* New York: Harper and Row, 1971, pp. 220 and 221.
6. L. Thomas Hopkins, *Interaction: The Democratic Process*. Boston: D.C. Heath, 1941.

2

Application of Philosophies of Education

In addition to the study of the broader philosophical schools of thought such as realism, idealism, experimentalism, existentialism, Thomism, and Marxism, each of these educational philosophies, past and present, can be clarified into a rather coherent applicable whole.

Realism and the Measurement Movement

Realism is very much inherent when states and districts establish and mandate that a precise list of behaviourally stated objectives need to be achieved by students. The real world, according to realists, can be known as it truly is, in whole or in part. Thus, specific objectives that students need to achieve can be identified. These objectives can be elected and placed in a set for all students to attain. Either a student, as a result of instruction, does or does not attain any one specific end. The precision of objectives identified and placed into a set for all students to achieve emphasizes knowing the real world as it truly is (the end of instruction) in whole or in part. Elements of certainty of knowledge are inherent in realism. The degree of being certain is reflected within the state emphasizing a core of objectives being available for student attainment. The same is true for district-wide mandated objectives (instructional management systems).

The realist then is rather certain which objectives students are to attain. They may also be certain as to which levels (percentile rank, and standard deviations above and below the mean pupils are achieving at). A realist tends not to like qualitative terms such as good, average, or poor. Rather he/she wants to know exactly how many test items a person responded correctly to and how many were missed. Exactness and precision in numerical results in reporting student progress is important.

A realist communicates to students prior to instruction what is to be acquired from a lesson to be presented. Thus, for example, prior to instruction, the teacher states to students, "After we are through with today's lesson, you will be able to list in writing three causes of World War II." The teacher then teaches causes of World War II. A variety of learning opportunities may be utilized such as reading activities and audio-visual aid experiences. After instruction, the teacher measures if students individually have/have not attained the stated objective. The teacher can be certain if learners have been successful in terms of having attained the measurably stated objective. Students knew prior to instruction what was expected to them in terms of content to be mastered. The measurement procedure harmonized with the stated objective. The learning activities were aligned with the predetermined objectives announced to students prior to instruction. Both the measurement technique and the activities for learning were valid in that each harmonized with the predetermined objective. Content validity stresses that which has been taught can be written as test items. Test items are not valid if they do not pertain to what has been taught. Reliability in testing is inherent if students' test results measure consistently be it test-retest, split half, or alternative forms.

Realism and the testing-measurement movement is one philosophy of instruction. They are not absolutes even though a state may mandate that these objectives must be emphasized in teaching-learning situations within a classroom.

Implications from realism in the curriculum include the following:

1. precise, measurably stated objectives are written prior to instruction;
2. the teacher announces prior to teaching what students are to learn as a result of instruction;
3. activities for instruction should contain only which is stated in the objective;
4. appraisal procedures emphasize evaluating student achievement in terms of what was stated in the objective (s);
5. sequence of activities provided for students is planned by the teacher;
6. tests are valid if they measure what is stated in the objectives;
7. activities, are valid if they align directly with the stated objectives;
8. techniques of appraisal need to align very precisely with the objectives.

Pertaining to realism, Bowyer[1] wrote:

> We have noted that there are different forms of naturalism and of idealism. The same is true to realism, which makes it difficult to pinpoint the distinguishing features of realism and to define the realist point of view. One element that the various forms of realism do have in common is a rejection of the idealist theory of knowledge that the various qualities of experience depend upon a knower for their existence. Realists believe that the universe is composed of real entities that exist in themselves. These entities can be known, and their existence is not dependent upon a knower or perceiver. Although realists can agree on this point, they do not all degree when they attempt to build a metaphysical system. Here their views range from pluralism to dualism to monism.
>
> The realist's epistemological views include epistemological monism where it is held that objects are presented in consciousness, and epistemological dualism where objects are

thought to be represented. The monists define mind as a relation between the organism and an object, while the dualists identify the mind more closely with the organisms. Realists do have a common tendency to view the world as the mechanism described by the physical sciences, and they generally believe in determinism, in orderliness in the universe, and in the objectivity of science. The unifying thesis of realism is that knowledge is thought to have a universal character and comes to man through his sensory capacity. The realists have a confidence in their assertions about reality and value which is most disconcering to pragmatists.

Idealism and Subject Matter Approaches of Instruction

Idealists tend to be very academic and rigorous in the teaching of subject matter. They emphasize cognitive objectives much more so than affective (attitudinal) or psychomotor (use of muscles and eye-hand coordination) in teaching-learning situations. Meaning, understanding, and depth learning of subject matter are important to idealists. Vital subject matter, carefully selected, needs to be taught to students. The student in acquiring subject matter in ongoing lessons is to move from the finite (limited) to the Infinite Being. Ideas are important to attain in an idealist's curriculum. The ideal is also salient to achieve in terms of moral standards and values.

The teacher emphasizing idealism as a philosophy of education stresses the selection of subject matter for student attainment which assists in forming vital concepts and generalizations. Objectives of instruction need to reflect worthwhile concepts and generalizations. Depth teaching of specifics assists students to form and develop viable universal ideas. The use of behaviourally stated objectives for instruction would be frowned upon by the idealist teacher. Content would become too fragmented with the realist's position of testing and measuring reflecting precise measurably stated objectives. Rather, the idealist in emphasizing an idea centered curriculum desires that students relate subject matter acquired so that intense learning transpires. Thus if students are studying causes of World War II, each cause would be studied thoroughly and not merely listed. Causes come in sequence and are complex to appraises. Viewing and analysing each cause takes time. After analysing, relating or synthesizing ideas takes time in order to emphasize intensity, not survey teaching. Students are to be evaluated in progress as to how much vital subject matter has been acquired.

The use of the mind or intellect is salient for students to utilize in analysing and synthesizing subject matter knowledge. Mental development is stressed as students learn, achieve, and develop.

Implications from idealism is a philosophy of education for the curriculum include the following:

1. intellectual, not attitudinal nor psychomotor, goals come first in teaching-learning situations;
2. quality textbooks, workbooks, and selected audio-visual materials which aid in intellectual achievement should be utilized as learning activities to achieve stated goals for students;
3. evaluation techniques should stress appraisal of vital subject matter acquired by students;
4. depth teaching of subject matter is salient to guide learners to attain vital facts, concepts, and generalizations. Survey approaches are not acceptable;
5. the will of the student is needed to attain worthwhile subject matter. Interest of students, alone, is not adequate for students to achieve, attain, and develop well. Students must want to learn;
6. students need to experience vital subject matter to prepare for the future life of an adult. Education is preparation for adult responsibilities, not present day situations in being a child;
7. learners need to develop from a finite (limited) being toward the Absolute or the Infinite (unlimited being). The Absolute may also be referred to as God;
8. a quality general education programme, consisting of major academic disciplines, is a must for all students.

Pertaining to idealism, Bigge[2] wrote:

> The heart of idealism is the belief that basic reality consists of ideas, thoughts, minds or substantive selves, not physical matter. Since priority is given to minds, minds have bodies, but bodies do not have minds. Idealism usually carries with its view the idea of the subsistence (the superexistence) of God, who also is basically mind or self. The universe is an expression of intelligence and will, its order is due to an eternal, spiritual reality. For idealists, people are good-active substantive minds; they are absolutely real selves endowed with free will or genuine moral choice. This philosophy has ancient roots; it dates back to Socrates (469-399 B.C.) and Plato (427-347 B.C.);
>
> Idealism really is idea-ism. The source of this title is based on Platonic thought. For Plato, ideas alone were genuinely real; they consisted of immaterial essences. That which people perceive is a shadow of reality; each thing that they perceive gets its existence from its Thingness; an Idea. A book is a book because of its being more or less imperfect replica of Bookness. A women is a woman because she is a replica of Womanness. Plato's assumed world of "eternal verities" consisted of the True, the Good, and the Beautiful;
>
> We can trace the development of idealism by listing some of the leading philosophers who have contributed to this position and stating a leading idea that each has contributed to the philosophy Socrates believed that children are born with knowledge already in their minds, but that they needed help to recall this innate knowledge. Plato contributed the idea of Ideas, which are the universal forms of all existing and are the essence of reality. St. Augustine (350-430) held a dualistic (mind-body) theory of humanity within which the mind or soul is the seat of the force of goodness.

Experimentalism and Subject Matter

Experimentalists believe that subject matter is instrumental to the solving of problems. Experimentalists oppose the realist position of students learning subject matter to achieve specific, behaviourally stated objectives. They also oppose the idealist position of students learning content in depth without relationship to identified problems needing solutions.

Experimentalists believe that identified problems should come from students. These problems are life-like and come from the societal arena in which human beings interact with others. Thus, within an ongoing unit, a student may have raised the question "What caused World War II?" The problem is intrinsic to the learner. A desire comes from within the student to receive needed information. The problem and the student are integrated, not separate entities. Interest in the problem and effort put forth to solve it also reveal unity, not separateness. Within a unit, students in a committee secure and utilize data sources to find the necessary information. A variety of sources need to be utilized to secure answers to the identified problems. Next, a hypothesis (tentative answers) are developed in directly relating to "What caused World War II?" Additional reference sources may be utilized to appraise the accuracy of the original hypothesis. The hypothesis stands on its own merits and is accepted, modified, or refuted as additional evidence warrants.

Implications for experimentalism in developing the curriculum are the following:

1. students with teacher encouragement need to select life-like problems within a contextual teaching-learning situation;
2. a variety of reference sources, directly related to the problem, should be utilized to assist in solving the identified problem(s);
3. a hypothesis, an answer to the problem, need to be developed by students, based on the knowledge acquired from utilizing the diverse reference sources;
4. diverse tests in life-like situations need to be utilized to evaluate each hypothesis;
5. the hypothesis may need revision if evidence warrants. Additional problems may also be selected by students within any teaching-learning situation.

Pertaining to John Dewey's philosophy of experimentalism, Meyer[3] wrote:

> All this, of course, depends in no small way on thinking. For Dewey, however, thinking becomes significant only when applied to life situations. It is, he has said, "an instrumentality used by man in adjusting himself to the practical situations of life." Or

> to phrase it more simply, human beings think in order to live. Because of this stimulus, which has its basis in biology and sociology, it is impossible—it is absurd—to interpret life in a systematic and abstract way. Since, moreover, Dewey holds that life is in constant flux, it is impossible to solve problems with any degree of finalty for the problems of tomorrow will be different from those of today;
>
> As for the problem of knowledge, Dewey believes that knowledge is experience and that true experience is functional. What is this thing for? What is its use? Is a coal mine a physical deposit or does it have function? And if so, what is it? Such are the questions that help to give meaning to one's experience; but such questions cannot be answered without antecendent action. Action must precede knowledge. Whatever knowledge we possess has resulted from our activities, our efforts to survive, to obtain food, shelter, and clothing. Only that which has been organized into our disposition so as to enable us to adapt our environment to our needs and to adapt our aims and desires to the situation in which we exist is really knowledge.

Existentialism and Subject Matter

Existentialists encourage the concept of openness in teaching-learning situations. Thus, in an ongoing unit of study, students select what to learn from among alternatives. A learning center philosophy may be used. One learning center, from among several, has a task on a card whereby the student may select to find information on "What caused World War II to happen?" With four or five activities on each task card and, perhaps, twelve centers in the classroom, a student may omit what does not possess perceived purpose. A student might or might not select to find information on "What caused World War II to occur?" He/she may also choose reference sources to utilize individually or within a committee to secure answers to the chosen identified problem. The learner selects the task (be it problem solving or other activity) to complete. Alternative routes should always be available other that the activities listed on task cards. Thus, student-teacher planning might be used in agreed upon activities for the former to complete. As many choices as possible need to be given to students where existentialism, as a philosophy, is utilized in the classroom. The student, not the teacher, is the focal point in the classroom.

Subject matter tends to be subjective, not objective to an existentialist. Moral standards and values need to be discussed within subject matter content. Morality and values might well be appraised as to utilizing wars to resolve conflicts. Learners need to view alternative approaches in resolving disagreements among nations, groups, and individuals.

Existentialists emphasize the importance of individuals continually making choices in the school curriculum and in the curriculum of life. If a person allows other to make decisions for oneself, this also represents a choice. However, to be an authentic human being, the person individually must do the choosing and making of decisions.

There are no predetermined objectives for individuals to achieve when entering the arena of life. Thus, open-ended situations exist in life to develop one's personal aspirations and goals. Since many, many options exist in terms of objectives for individual pursuit, feelings of anxiety and tension may result. The personal moral choices or decisions made may end in desirable consequences. They may also result in failure and alienation. Situation in life are not rational, but appear to be absurd in many cases.

Implications for teachers pertaining to existentialism in the curriculum can include the following:

1. pupils individually must be given ample opportunities to choose objectives and learning experiences;
2. knowledge is subjective; thus the arts, values clarification, literature, history, philosophy, and music should receive adequate emphasis in the curriculum;
3. individuals in the school-class setting must be encouraged to make personal commitments in life. Moral judgements made by individuals in a free environment are an ultimate goal in teaching and learning;
4. the individual pupil is a chooser and thus determines criteria and standards in life. The teacher definitely does not dictate values for pupils' acceptance. Nor does the teacher determine means and ends of learning for

pupils. Certainly, the teacher should not expect pupils to accept rationality existing in life's situations.

Jean-Paul Sartre[4] wrote the following:

> Man is nothing else but what he makes of himself. Such is the first principle of existentialism. It is also what is called subjectivity, the name we are labelled with when charges are brought against us. But what do we mean by this, if not that man has a greater dignity than a stone or table? For we mean that man first exists, that is, that man first of all is the being who hurls himself toward a future and who is conscious of imagining himself as being in the future. Man is at the start a plan which is aware of itself, rather than a patch of moss, a piece of garbage, or a cauliflower; nothing exists prior to this plan; there is nothing in heaven; man will be what he will have planned to be. Not what he will want to be. Because by the word "will" we generally mean a conscious decision, which is subsequent to what we have already made of ourselves. I may want to belong to a political party, write a book, get married; but all that is only a manifestation of an earlier, more spontaneous choice that is called "will." But if existence really does precede essence, man is responsible for what he is. Thus, existentialism's first move is to make every man aware of what he is and to make the full responsibility of his existence rest upon him. And when we say that a man is responsible for himself, we do not only mean that he is responsible for his own individuality, but that he is responsible for all men.

Perennialism and Subject Matter

Perennialists seek vital ideas of great minds of the past to select subject matter for students to learn. Thus, for example, Plato's *Republic* might well be selected as a classic for students to read. The content can be simplified for young readers in terms of levels of complexity of abstract words. Reading materials utilized should be on the understanding level of students. Best it is to read the *Republic* in the original writing. Students may then understand, for example, what Plato meant by justice in his ideal republic or nation. Persons would be classified then into three categories or workers—rulers, warriors, and artisans. Formal schooling of all would cull out first the artisans, next the warriors, and those remaining would be trained and educated as government officials of the republic. Governmental officials represent the highest status and are truly philosopher-kings. Students could learn about perfection (the Forms or heaven) as well as the planet earth which contains its many imperfections according to Plato. Other great books of the western world also contain vital ideas for students.

Implications for perennialism in the curriculum might well include the following:

1. that which is essential for each student to acquire represents basic knowledge and has been deemed salient throughout the decades and centuries;
2. the mind or mental development comes first in teaching-learning situations, not the affective or psychomotor domains;
3. a common body of knowledge is available to students through a study of the great books;
4. general education needs to be acquired, prior to the selection of a vocation, occupation, or profession;
5. communication with others is possible through essential ideas acquired from the great books. A common body of knowledge is available then to all students;
6. vital content is acquired which has been tested in time and space. Trivia is then weeded out;
7. achievement in the liberal arts assist one to explore knowledge and discover his/her niche in life.

Pertaining to perennialism, O'Neill[5] wrote:

> Accordingly, educational intellectualism tends to be past-oriented and to emphasize stability—the continuity of the great, enduring ideas—over change. In general, the eternal truths are best represented in the abiding masterworks of the world's greatest minds as these are conveyed through the cultural heritage of mankind. The overall goal of education is to identify, preserve and transmit essential Truth (that is, the central principles that govern the underlying meaning and significance of life). More specifically, the intermediate role of the school as a particular social institution is to teach the students how to think (that is, how to reason) and to transmit the best thought (the enduring wisdom) of the past.

In contemporary education, philosophical conservation expresses itself primarily as educational intellectualism, which encompasses two basic variations: philosophical intellectualism and theological intellectualism. Philosophical intellectualism is probably best represented in America today by such individuals as Robert Maynard Hutchins and Mortimer Adler, who are both primarily concerned with metaphysical wisdom in the traditional Aristotelian sense and who both tend to place great emphasis on traditional "liberal arts' education in the spirit of the "Great Books."

Thomism, Catholicism, and Subject Matter

Thomists view a study of literature, grammar, history, geography, political science, mathematics, physics, chemistry, biology, art, music, and physical education as a part of the liberal arts curriculum. The liberal arts are emphasized for their own sake and not necessarily instrumental to the solving of problems. Contemplation and reason are prime objectives for students to attain in the liberal arts. The liberal arts need to emphasize correct thinking which is contemplation (mediating) and reason.

Human being can be separated completely from animal life in that the former has soul which animals do not have. The soul ultimately unites with God, whereas the physical features, after this life has been completed, return to dust. Quality liberal education develops the soul and intellect. A human being's destiny is not confined to the planet Earth. Rather, the hereafter is highly important. Faith, not merely empiricism, is salient for any person. The faith pertains to belief in God, Jesus, and the Holy Spirit—a triune God. Supernaturalism and miracles do occur. Natural law alone is not sovereign in the universe. Revealed truth from God is important. Revealed truth may well be the highest form of TRUTH. Thomism adheres to universal truths which are eternal in time and place. Students need to learn and accept concepts of obedience, humility, sacrifice, docility, and self control. Faith in God, immortality, the grace of God, and the soul are key concepts in the Catholic philosophy of education. The individuals' relationship with God is the most important factor in Thomism as a philosophy of education.

Education of students needs to emphasize what human beings are and what their destiny is. Humans are not physical alone, but are spiritual beings possessing reason and faith in God. Being responsible members in society (secular responsibilities), accepting family duties, and earning a living are further goals to emphasize in the educational arena. Being of service to others in society stresses charity or love. Faith, hope and love are three enduring values to stress in Catholic education.

Implications for the curriculum with Thomism as a philosophy of education may well include the following:

1. the teachings of the Catholic church come first in education;
2. the liberal arts, physical education, and social development are also salient. (Jesus grow in wisdom, and in stature, and in favour with God and man.);
3. each student needs to grow in faith toward the Catholic church, in hope for the future , and in love for others;
4. subject matter is acquired for its own sake and hopefully for application and use also;
5 human beings are at the apex of creation, well above that of animal life;
6. reason and contemplation are two vital concepts to emphasize in Catholic education;
7. each person's relationship with God is primary;
8. mastery of the liberal arts assists in developing the rational being.

Wahlquist[6] wrote the following on the thinking of Geoffrey O'Connell:

> O'Connell, Catholic idealist, is disturbed by the atheistic note in the writings of Dewey, Kilpatrick, and Rugg. All three take the position that man is continuous with nature, confine his destiny to the earth, and eliminate any trace of the supernatural. He finds evidence of a denial of the "abiding faith," fixed and absolute, and a denial of God, supernaturalism, revelation, Christianity. Moreover, these pragmatists deny the concept of moral law as something externally or internally fixed. Dewey's confession of whole hearted naturalism is given much attention. Kilpatrick is accused of indoctrinating immature teachers with the concept of

a man-centered universe, where morals are pragmatic, experimental, and relative; hence, his concern for methodology, which is to snatch the schools from the Church. Even the virtues of sacrifice, humility, self-restraint, docility, and obedience are said to be challenged by Kilpatrick. Although Rugg finds a place for something more than problem solving, his creative artists are imbued with the naturalism of Emerson and Whitman. Rugg is said to regard Christianity as a system of bondage, a medieval culture, anesthised by myth and superstition. Moreover, he is especially biased toward revealed religion.

Marxism and Subject Matter

This world is the only one that individuals will ever experience. The here and the now alone are important. After each person has breathed his/her last breath on this planet, there is no more life for that individual. Since this life in the here and the now alone is salient, each person needs to learn to acquire the necessities of life. However, the collective, not the individual, should aid in obtaining adequate food, clothing, shelter, and other necessities. Each person, will be a worker in society. The ideal is the worker in a collective society. Socially useful labour should be experienced by all in the school setting. The traditional general educational/liberal arts curriculum is not adequate. Rather, vocational education needs to be fused and implemented into the curriculum. Work has always been performed by human beings since the beginning of civilization.

A sharing of the world's goods and service is necessary. The elite, the wealthy, owners, and managers should contribute to the world of work and labour. They, too often, have usurped the profit that would be due to the workers. The worker is of central importance in Marxist philosophy.

Marx believed that no individual lives unto the self, but is a social being. The cohesive group, not the self, is important. Each individual behaves with reference to the times he/she is born in. Thus a person is a product of the times, or environment he/she exists and lives in.

Causes in life are not mechanical, but reveal creativity and uniqueness. Causes will effect diverse facets of society differently. Even theatres may have a response which is creative to a cause. Art, music, philosophy, science, the social sciences, and mathematics may each respond differently to a cause or causes. Each response acts on its very own, not in a mechanical stimulus-response way. Much creativity is in evidence in the thesis, antithesis, synthesis philosophy of life, accepted by Karl Marx.

Marx attempted to discover the earliest activity engaged in by human beings. The earliest activity was labour. Since humans are social beings, the collective in work performed was important. The means of production of goods and services must be the collective, not the individual. Struggles between workers and owners lead to change. Competition then emphasizes changes in society, not stability.

With change, the status quo is challenged. The thesis emphasizes what is at present. The antithesis stresses the opposite school of thought. Competition and class struggles make for opposing positions, such as thesis and antithesis. Owners and workers have conflicting points of view. What is produced by workers is controlled by the owners. It is the worker, however through time and effort, that has produced the products. Clashes are bound to occur between owners and workers. (thesis and antithesis). A new level of operation in attempting to resolve the thesis and antithesis results in the synthesis. Owners have emphasized that workers in their miserable plight will receive their rewards in the hereafter or heaven, not in the here and now. Thus Marx emphasized religion as being the opiate of the people.

Implications for education and the curriculum of Karl Marx's writing might be the following:

1. students need to develop values of egalitarianism. Factory owners alienate workers which cause the latter to be more like animals who eat, drink and procreate. With a classless society, each worker may feel less of alienation and perceive purpose in life;
2. positive attitudes need development by students toward the world of work. Pride in work is an important objective for student attainment;
3. proper balance in education needs to exist between vocational and academic education. Neither is superior

to the other. Vocational experiences need integration with labour and the world of work;

4. objectives of instruction need to emphasize the history of labour and work. The labour and work arena was the first incident in the history of humankind;
5. pride and enjoyment in the vocational arena are important. Students need to feel successful in work experiences in the curriculum;
6. change as a concept should be expected by students. The triad of thesis, antithesis, and synthesis is reality. Changes may well be revolutionary;
7. excursions into the community for students are necessary. Thus school and society are two concepts (thesis and antithesis) which need harmonizing with a synthesis;
8. a concrete to abstract or near to far (expanding environment) sequence in the curriculum should be experienced by all students.

Pertaining to the dialected materialism of Karl Marx, Wayper[7] wrote:

> Nowhere unfortunately, does Marx tell us what he means by "materialism." But at least he makes it plain that his materialism is dialectical not mechanical. In mechanical materialism evolution is the path taken by material things under the pressure of their environment. In dialectical materialism, evolution is the development of matter from within, environment helping or hindering, but neither originating the evolutionary process nor capable of preventing it from reaching its inevitable goal. Matter, to the dialectical materialist, is active nor passive, and moves by an inner necessity of its nature. Therefore dialectical materialism is more interested in motion than in matter, in a viral energy within matter inevitably driving it towards perfect human society just as Hegel's demi-urge drove forward to the perfect realization of Spirit. As Engels said: "The dialectical method grasps things and their images, ideas, essentially in their sequence, their movement, their birth and death.

Summary

Each philosophy of education has unique uses and applications. Realists stress a behavioural psychology with its predetermined objectives written prior to instruction. After teaching learners, the teacher measures if students have been successful in goal attainment. Either a student has or has not achieved an objective. Students may know the real world in and of itself through specifics, such as measurably stated objectives, with ultimate knowledge of the whole.

Idealism stresses that students acquire vital subject matter in an idea centered curriculum. Ideas consist of concepts and generalizations for students to acquire. Concepts and generalizations as universals reveal the open-endedness of subject matter achieved, not in measurable terms as realists would advocate. The mind or spiritual part of a person becomes paramount to develop in teaching-learning situations.

Experimentalists place major emphasis upon students being successful identifiers and solvers of problems. An open ended learning environment is needed for students to engage in problems solving activities. Thus within a contextual situation, problems are identified and attempted solutions made in a life-like situation. With continuous change, new problems arise which need solutions in the world of experience.

Existentialism believes in choices and decisions made by the student within a highly flexible environment. The individual is responsible for acts and deeds, with no one else to blame for mistakes made due to freedom involving closing from among alternatives. To be human is to make sequential selections from within a highly open-ended curriculum.

Perennialism and its advocates recommend students experience general education for all, from the elementary years through the baccalaureate degree level, consisting of the Great Books emphasizing enduring subject matter from the past. Content from present day writers have not had the test of their ideas surviving time and place. Ideas of great thinkers, a study of history and geography, mathematics, and general science stress that which is permanent, not transitory.

Thomism harmonizes Christian thought with that of Aristotle. Among others, parallels between the two philosophies include a first cause which is *God* to the Catholic church and a Prime Mover according to Aristotle. The official theology of

Catholicism blends the thinking of the church (Bible) with Aristotelian philosophy. God, the Church, and the hereafter receive primary emphasis in Catholic Philosophy of education.

With Marxism, ultimate control of the means of production and distribution of goods and services rests with workers. With a triad of thesis, antithesis, and synthesis, workers ultimately become the dominant force in society. Owners and managers become obsolute as an institution. The state then will ultimately wither away.

REFERENCES

1. Bowyer, Carlton H., *Philosophical Perspectives for Education.* Glenview Illinois: Scott, Foresman and Company, 1970, p. 17.
2. Bigge, Morris L., *Educational Philosophies for Teachers.* Columbus, Ohio: Charles E. Merrill Publishing Company, 1982, pp. 25-26.
3. Meyer, Adoph E., *The Development of Education in the Twentieth Century.* Englewood Cliffs, New Jersey: Prentice Hall, Inc., 1949, pp. 42-43.
4. Alston, William P. and Brandt, Richard B., *The Problems of Philosophy.* Third Edition. Boston: Allyn and Bacon, Inc., 1978, pp. 257 and 258.
5. O'Neill, William F., *Educational Ideologies.* Santa Monica, California: Goodyear Publishing Company, Inc., 1981, p. 168.
6. Wahlquist, John T., *The Philosophy of American Education.* New York: Ronald Press Company, 1942, pp. 76 and 77.
7. Wayper, C.L., *Political Thought.* New York: Philosophical Library Inc., 1954, pp. 199 and 200.

3

A History of Philosophical Perspectives

Diverse schools of philosophy tend to have a long history. Realism, idealism, experimentalism, existentialism, Thomism and Marxism have histories that provide sequence in understanding modern philosophies of education.

John Locke, Johann Friedrich Herbart, and Realism

John Locke (1632-1704) had selected excellent ideas pertainng to teaching and learning. Locke believed that children should learn by example, rather than through lecture and doctrine. Thus the modeling approach was important to Locke. Teachers, parents, and others in society need to set a positive example for the young. Children learn from watching others. What is observed by children should assist in developing good individuals in society.

In acquiring the ability to speak a foreign language, Locke believed that children should learn by speaking and interacting with others. In Locke's day, foreign languages were taught with endless drill and repetition. Interest in learning was then negated. Learning should be enjoyable to children. Physical punishment, according to Locke, should not be in evidence. Too frequently in Locke's day, school's were places of whippings, torture, and sarcasm when teachers dealt with students. Students then feared the teacher, the school, and education.

John Locke's theory of education emphasized the concepts of sensation and reflection. Sensation stressed the use of the senses in learning. Seeing, hearing, touching, testing, and smelling represent five senses in learning. After sensation, individuals reflect upon that which had been acquired. With reflection, students doubted, willed, accepted, rejected and modified related content from sensation.

Pertaining to Locke's sensation and reflection concepts, Bowyer[1] wrote:

> According to Locke, there are only two legitimate sources of ideas, the sense and reflection upon the material of the sense and reflection itself. The greatest source of ideas is sensation which conveys distinct perceptions of things into the mind. In this manner, sensible qualities such as colour, softness, bitterness, and sweetness are produced. Reflection the perception of the way our mind operates with the ideas it has received from the senses, can be called an internal sense. The ideas furnished by reflection are things such as thinking, doubting, believing, reasoning, and willing. Thus, there is no reason to believe that the soul could possibly think before it receives impressions by way of the senses. Locke suggests that doubters search their own thinking to discover, as he is sure they will, that all of their ideas have come either from their senses or from reflections upon material that has been provided by the senses. Again, Locke refers to the child to prove the point that ideas grow in proportion to sense experiences and that as reflection upon sensible ideas increases, the faculties of judging and reasoning are developed.

John Locke emphasized for broad goals of learning. The first goal was virtue. To be virtuous individuals, one lives a decent life. Refraining from evil stresses virtue. Locke's second goal was wisdom. With wisdom, there is foresight in determining appropriate choices to make in life. The wise person knows in advance which are the better choices, from among alternatives. Third, Locke has good breeding as a goal. The well bred person has good manners and works well with others Locke was critical of "sheepish bashfulness" that certain people exhibited. Thus shyness and awkwardness in behaviour need to be avoided. Fourth, Locke stressed knowledge as being an objective to achieve. Locke realized he himself was a bookish person and liked academic knowledge. However, Locke believed virtue, wisdom, and breeding to be more salient objectives.

John Locke believed the 'environment to be highly important in teaching and learning. The mind was like a blank sheet at birth, according to Locke. The environment then imprinted upon the mind. Thus sensation and reflection occured. Mind being a blank sheet at birth is the Tabula Rasa theory. Later educators, such as Johann Friedrich Herbart (1776-1841) followed the Tabula Rasa theory in developing psychologies and philosophies of instruction. Students need to emulate good models in society so that imprinting of what is observed and said occurs on the mind.

In Locke's day, many educators believed in the "Hardening process." Here the student would experience unpleasant situations, such as leaky shoes and long periods of inclement whether in the out-of-doors, to make for a stronger person and thus survive in life. The hardening process concept indicates influences of the time upon John Locke's educational thinking.

Locks believed that education was a process, more so than a product. Thus educating the student involved developing good habits, training for morality and proper moral standards, disciplining the self, and attaining good habits. Locke believed strongly in "a sound mind in a sound body." Proper diet, exercise, and hardening of the body are important. Good manners and habits come from quality teaching and learning. Rewards should be given for good acts whereas appropriate punishment should follow in sequence to bad acts. Reason must be used by the child to curb negative influences. Education should help a person to become a reasoning individual. Locke believed that a study of mathematics would develop reasoning ability within the person. Locke[2] had tremendous faith in education, as is indicated by the following from his book *Some Thoughts Concerning Education:*

> A sound mind in a sound body, is a short, but full description of a happy state in this world; he that has these two, has little more to wish for; and he that wants either of them, will be but little the better for anything else. Men's happiness, or misery, is most part of their own making. He whose mind directs not

wisely, will never take the right way; and he whose body is crazy and feeble, will never be able to advance in it. I confess, there are some men's constitutions of body and mind so vigorous, and well framed by nature, that they need not much assistance from others; but, by the strength of their natural genius, they are from their cradles, carried towards what is excellent; and, by the privilege of their happy constitutions, are able to do wonders. But examples of this kind are but few; and I think I may say that, of all the men we meet with, nine parts of ten are what they are, good or evil, useful or not, by their education. It is that which makes the great difference in mankind. The little, or almost insensible, impressions or our tender infancies, have very important and lasting consequences; and there it is, as in the fountains of some rivers, where a gentle application of the hand turns the flexible waters into channels, the make them take quite contrary courses; and by this little direction, given them at first, in the source, they receive different tendencies, and arrive at least at very remote and distant places.

Knowledge of the Bible is important for all, according to Locke. Whatever is taught generally be enjoyable and pleasant. Locke opposed scholasticism as a philosophy of teaching for his day. Scholasticism was a remnant of the Middle Ages whereby opposing sides would quote the writings of church fathers pertaining to a dispute. No one was to go beyond the writings of the church fathers. Creativity certainly was lacking in scholastic methods of education. Locke opposed the involved formalism. He favoured more modern approaches emphasizing a psychology of learning. Virtue, wisdom, and breeding as traits to develop were more important than book learning for Locke.

John Locke emphasized his plans for education for the upper class. Educating the gentleman's son was his goal in writing *An Essay Concerning Human Understanding.* The gentleman was to be concerned with government, the world, and the further development of the individual. The polished person should know geography, history, and politics. A broadly educated person was desired, including being highly knowledgeable in the academic areas of physics, mathematics, and modern languages.

Locke believed more in developing proper attitudes within children for learning rather than the subject matter acquired. The tutor is to develop within the child a love for learning content as well as to prize highly the opportunities for attaining subject matter. A survey approach to learning was emphasized by John Locke. Later, the child could learn in depth what is of personal interest from the surveyed content. Studying a variety of subject matter. A survey content. Studying a variety of subject matter areas rather than a single one is preferable. A student needs to be broadly, not narrowly, educated. Open-mindedness is preferable to narrow-mindedness. Freedom of thought is to be emphasized.

Pertaining to Locke's emphasis upon attitudinal development within students, Ulich[3] wrote:

> Starting from the conception that knowledge has to foster, rather than to impede, the growth of an all-rounded personality, Locke demanded a method of education apt to encourage initiative, independent judgement, observation, and critical use of reason. He wanted languages taught by conversation, not by grammatical exercises and memorization; generally speaking, he preferred learning by doing to learning by imitation. Consequently, his plans for a curriculum favoured such subjects as the sciences, geography, astronomy, and mathematics for introducing the young into the world of nature; the Bible, history, and chronology for developing in the young a sense of morality and human affairs and the greatness of their nation; accounting as a requisite for good husbandry; and the vernacular and modern languages as means for communication. Of the ancient languages, he wanted Greek dropped from the ordinary programme of a gentleman's education; he wanted Latin Taught by speaking it, like modern languages, and used merely as an instrument, not as an end in itself.

Locke was opposed to humanism, prevalent in his day. Humanists placed much emphasis on learning many languages such as Greek and Hebrew. Locke felt too much time was wasted by students in laborious ways of studying these languages. Then too, the teacher's rod was used very frequently to discipline children when drill and more drill were emphasized in learning the diverse foreign languages. Locke would do away with the Study of Greek, except for university students desiring to study this language. Latin would be taught but not to drill students to have the eloquence of Cicero, and ancient Roman orator and statesman. Teaching grammar was to be greatly minimized. Grammar, during the Middle Ages period of time, had been emphasized much as a salient academic discipline. The disputations or scholasticism from the Middle Ages where to be eliminated. Locke disliked disputations due to students becoming dogmatic and not arriving at worthwhile subject matter.

Locke denied the existence of innate ideas. Rather, the environment (education) imprinted itself upon the mind as a blank sheet (the Tabula Rasa theory). He did believe in mental faculties of the mind. Thus, the mind was divided into categories (faculties). Each faculty could be strengthened through learning. The mind, according to Locke, could be divided into parts. Each part (category) through teaching and learning would become stronger and better developed. Mind was conceived to be like a muscle. With proper exercise the muscles in the body can be strengthened. Also, the mind with mental exercises can be made stronger. With mind like a blank sheet at birth, the educational environment imprints its simple and complex ideas.

Simple ideas come from:

1. the use of the five senses;
2. reflection, such as comparing, doubting, believing, willing, contrasting, and judging;
3. both sensation and reflection, such as ideas about unity, pleasure, existence, and power.

Complex ideas come from:

1. a comparison of simple ideas;
2. a unity of simple ideas;
3. a combination and multiplicity of content or subject matter.

John Locke divided ideas into primary and secondary qualities. Ideas become a part of the person and are inside of the individual, through learning and not innately. Locke emphasized objective reality and the real world of external objects. Primary qualities are real and reside within the external world. The mind then receives a duplicate of the real world. The theory of correspondence is involved in that what the mind perceives is the actual, real world as it truly is and exists. Examples of primary qualities are the number of actual objects involved, solids in and of themselves, movement of objects, objects in a stationary situation, as well as extension of real items in the environment.

Primary qualities give/provide information the five senses of seeing, hearing, testing, touching, and smelling. An animal then takes up space, a primary quality. The animal has colour which involves the sense of seeing, a secondary quality. Locke also emphasized a third quality, such as a solid (a primary quality) being heated to change the solid to a liquid or perhaps even a gas. Cause and effect were important in the thinking of John Locke. Primary qualities then affect each other.

There are selected implications which may be derived from the philosophy of John Locke. These include the following:

1. rich learning opportunities must be the right of all students since the environment (education) can make or break the individual. Richness in the curriculum imprints itself (Tabula Rasa) upon the minds of learners;
2. sense experiences provide the raw materials for student learning. Thus the teacher needs to utilize concrete materials heavily in teaching/learning situations. From the concrete, students might then utilize the senses in learning. Faculty psychology of John Locke would be outdated in that exercising the muscles in the body cannot be compared with mental growth and development. Faculty psychology and the theory of mental discipline has long been discredited;
3. teachers need to help students to react to sense impressions. Higher levels of thinking are then involved (reflection). The teacher needs to guide students to compare, contrast, believe and doubt that which was gained from use of the senses;
4. empirical methods of teaching should be emphasized. John Locke was an empiricist in that an objective external world existed in which the observer may

receive a duplicate (Tabula Rasa theory) of observations made.

John Locke unfortunately was to concerned much with the education of children from poor families. For the poor, Locke recommended students learning to weave baskets and cloth. The woven products are to be sold so that the individual could be self-supporting and eat watery soup and have a bellyful of bread. Wayper[4] wrote the following pertaining to Locke's thinking on upper/lower classes' role in government:

> The first and most important characteristic of Locke's state is that it exists for the people who form it, they do not exist for it. Repeatedly he insists that "the end of government" is "the good of community." "Political power," he says, "I take to be a right of making laws with penalties of death, and consequently all less penalties, for the regulating and preserving of property, and of employing the force of the community in the execution of such laws, and in the defence of the commonwealth from foreign injury, and all this only for the public good." The State, in fact, is a machine which we create for our good and run for our purposes, and it is both dangerous and unnecessary to speak of some supposed mystical good of State or country independent of the lives of individual citizens;
>
> Locke goes further and insists that all true States must be founded on consent. It is true that he assumes that a minority, will consent in all things to the rule of the majority, who have, he asserts, "a right to act and conclude the rest." It is true that he regards the consent of representatives as an adequate substitute for the consent of all. It is true that he is driven to admit that consent may be tacit rather than open and express, and that ultimately he is prepared to declare that a man gives tacit consent to a government by being simply within its territories. Nevertheless, it is both important and typical of him that he loses no opportunity of insisting the importance of consent and displays considerable mental ingenuity in proving that men have consented to obey their rulers when it is in their interest to do so, and that when those rulers act harmfully they are doing to without consent of their subjects.

John Locke clearly emphasized realist perspectives in philosophy Locke believed that each person was born with mind like a blank sheet (the Tubula Rasa theory). The environment imprints itself upon the minds of individuals from birth on to present times. The individual then tends to receive a replica of the real world as it truly is. Sensation, according to Locke, emphasizes receiving content from the real world through the use of the senses. Seeing, feeling, tasting, touching, and smelling provide sense data. After sensation has occured, reflection is in evidence. Thus, the sense data is acted upon through means of reflection. With reflection, the individual doubts, believes, wills, modifies, and refutes what was received through the senses. Thinking about that which was obtained as sense data stresses reflection.

To emphasize realism more thoroughly, John Locke believed in primary and secondary qualities. With primary qualities, reality existed in items and objectives perceived by the senses. Thus the number of items, movement, and shape reside within the objects. However, the colour, odor, softness or hardness, taste, and noises made of objective reside within the perceiver.

Locke believed strongly that children learn by example. The examples, not lectures, of the adult imprint upon the mind of the young. As a whole, Locke believed that learning activities should be enjoyable, not harsh or punitive. The enjoying of activities and experiences imprint or provide a duplicate copy to the mind.

Cubberley[5] wrote:

> Locke has set up as the aim of education the ideal of a physically sound gentleman. Rousseau had declared his aim to be to prepare his boy for life by developing naturally his inborn talents. Pestalozzi had sought to regenerate society by means of education, and to prepare children for society by a "harmonious training" of their "faculties." Herbart rejected alike the conventional-social education of Locke, the natural and unsociable education of Rosseau, and the faculty-psychology "conception" of education of Pestalozzi. Instead, he conceived the mind to be a unity, instead of being divided into "faculties," and the aim of education as broadly social rather than personal. The purposes of education, he said, was to prepare men to live properly in organized society, and hence the chief aim in education was not conventional fitness, natural development, mere knowledge, nor personal mental power, but personal character and social morality. This being the case, the educator should analyze the interests and occupations and social responsibilities of men as

they are grouped in organized society, and, from such analysis, deduce the means and methods of instruction. Man's interests, he said, come from two main sources—his contact with things in the environment (real things, sense-impressions), and from his relations with other human beings (social intercourse), His social responsibilities and duties are determined by the nature of the social organization of which he forms a part.

Johann Freidrich Herbart (1776-1841) was also a strong advocate of the Tabula Rasa theory of mind being like a blank sheet at birth. Herbart provided excellent examples in a psychology of learning whereby the Tabula Rasa theory was in evidence. Five steps of teaching advocated by Herbart and his followers where preparation, presentation, association, generalization, and application.

The step of preparation emphasizes reviewing with students what had been learned previously. The step of review changed ideas in the mind from being hazy to possessing clarity. Unless review is emphasized content lacks clearness and may be forgotten. Presentation, a second step of teaching, stresses new content presented by the teacher to learners. The new content needs to be understandable and meaningful.

The new is related to the content reviewed in the step of preparation. To prevent undue isolated items to accrue in the minds of students, Harbart advocated the step of association in teaching. Here, the teacher assists students to relate ideas to prevent small bits of information to clutter the mind. The isolated items hinder retention of what had been learned. Following the association of ideas, the teacher helps students to generalize. The broader ideas, or generalizations, cover the steps of preparation and presentation in the teaching of students. Harbart was a strong believer in step five of teaching which is application. Unless subject matter acquired is applied or used, rapid forgetting occurs. Johann Friedrich Herbart then developed a philosophy and psychology of teaching based on the Tabula Rasa theory.

Ulich[6] wrote the following pertaining to Herbart's beliefs:

> As we already know, good instruction uses the incentives inherent in interest. For this purpose the teacher must find out what kind of presentation and learning is commensurate with the

> child's capacity. Otherwise the school obstructs rather than assists the growth of the child's personality. On the other hand, every individual lives in society and must learn to comply with the objective standards and requirements characteristic of every civilization. The more advanced such a civilization is, the less can the individual be permitted simply to follow his bents and affections; rather, he must be able to direct them so that his individuality serves that civilization in and on which it thrives. Only in such ways can an individual be productive and feel himself free and happy.
>
> Hence there arise for the teacher, on the one hand, the obligation to cultivate the interest of the child, in order to stimulate his spontaneity; on the other hand, the need not only to cultivate the child's personal interests but to introduce him to the variety of human knowledge and experiences, in order to help him in the appreciation of the fundamental values of civilized societies. Such education, Herbart would call a "liberal education."

Numerous contributions were made by Johann Friedrich Herbart in developing teaching into a science rather than strictly an art. With five sequential steps of teaching to emphasize in preparing each lesson plan, Herbart had a specific order to stress in the act of teaching. Definite reasons were given by Herbart for advocating each step or sequence. It does make good sense to prepare pupils for the new learnings to be presented. Preparing meant reviewing, rehearsing, and recalling of previously acquired subject matter. Many good teachers today review with students subject matter that was taught previously, meaning yesterday or a few days ago. Otherwise, the human being may have little background information to explore, The writer believes quality teachers have always assisted students, using a variety of learning opportunities, to recall and to retain significant facts, concepts, and generalization acquired previously.

Excellent teachers realize that teaching and learning must go beyond review. Otherwise, how can students learn what is new and has not been experienced? Thus, new content needs to be presented to learners.

With too many new ideas presented in an isolated manner, the learner may have many difficulties in remembering what has been taught. Educational psychologist today state that knowledge taught as being related will be remembered longer than that taught in isolation. Herbart strongly stressed the significance of students being aided to associate, correlate, fuse, and relate the new subject matter taught (presentation) with older content reviewed (step of preparation).

Certainly out of the associations, it is important for students to generalize. Educational psychologies today emphasize the importance of students achieving order out of facts secured by relating the factual content to broader ideas such as generalizations or main ideas. The generalizations are supported by related facts. The accuracy of any valid generalization' can be checked, in general, with supporting specific items of information.

Lastly, Herbart advocated students utilizing that which had been learned. Principles of learning taken from the psychology of education would agree whole-heartedly. Unless knowledge is utilized, rapid forgetting generally occurs. No doubt, trivia in subject matter is minimized if knowledge is put to use in one way or another. Educators have strongly recommended that the useless, the unimportant, and the insignificant be weeded out. What does it profit any person to learn useless subject matter, skills, or attitudes? There is so much to learn and the finite being can only learn a small amount of what is available. One way to test the worth of learnings acquired is to attempt to put it to use.

Thus, Herbart advocated a science of instruction with the ordered steps of teaching to be put into a lesson plan. The sequential steps of teaching, namely preparation, presentation, association, generalization, and use in a lesson plan emphasized a consistent approach in teacher's developing lesson plans.

Herbart seemingly was clear on which objectives to emphasize in teaching students, namely to develop the moral being. There have been educators who were very open ended in stating goals for students to attain. There has been criticism, warranted or unwarranted, in instructors lacking objectives, adequately specific for student attainment.

Herbart is to be credited for emphasizing the interests of students in ongoing lessons. Otherwise, learnings can not reach the conscious levels of students.

Herbart in advocating mind as a blank sheet (Tabula Rasa) at birth assisted in dealing a death blow to the theory of mental discipline. In the mental discipline theory, traditional educators believed that subject matter to be learned by students be complex indeed! In fact, content was to be so difficult that students disliked what was beirg presented. Why? The mind was conceived to be like the human body. If the mind were exercised like muscles in the body, the former would become strengthened and strong. Any subject matter later might then be acquired by students, no matter how complicated.

Herbart disagreed with the theory of mental discipline in that "exercising its muscles" strengthen the mind, Rather, Herbart advocated securing learner interests when teaching. Also, relating new learnings to previous content acquired by the student would be opposite of exercising the muscles of the mind theory. By relating new content learned with previous ideas developed, Herbart emphasized a core curriculum in which subject matter from diverse academic disciplines are related.

Herbart was a great philosopher and psychologist in education. He developed and utilized his thinking in the training and education of teachers. There, no doubt, are always weaknesses in the thinking of any educator. Sometimes, the weakness are philosophical and pertain to differences in value systems, such as an activity centered teacher using a learning by doing approach for pupils as compared to a subject centered teacher. Both can be excellent instructors if individual differences among students are adequately provided for. Each learner needs to achieve optimally regardless of philosophical position taken in teaching students.

What then might be selected criticisms of the Herbartian method of teaching students.

1. John Dewey (1859-1952), late professor of Colombia University, believed that Herbart's five steps of teaching were too rigid and formal. He believed that teachers could become slavish imitators of these methods in stressing conformity behaviour of students. There are many educators who believe that Herbart meant the five steps to be followed in a flexible informal manner.

Herbart might even have emphasized four flexible sequences rather than five. These were the steps of clarity (meaningful learnings), association (relating new learnings received to those acquired previously), system (understanding specific items learned), and method (application of what has been learned).

2. Herbart also has been criticized in emphasizing the academic and abstract to the exclusion of the concrete and the vocational. There are educators who strongly advocate students learning that which has utilitarian values. Thus, what is learned has its usefulness in the real world of vocations and society. John Dewey would strongly emphasize this strand of thought. There is much to be said in favour of a curriculum emphasising practical learnings useful is the societal arena. Toward the other end of the continuum, Herbart would not be as symbolic in his educational philosophy as compared to Aristotle (384—322 BC). The latter emphasized the highest good in life to involve pure contemplation. The contemplating should be as much removed from the real world as possible. Thinking about pure ethics and morality completely in the abstract without practical application would involve Aristotle's highest level of behaviour which is contemplation.

3. Selected educators believe that the teacher dominates the classroom setting in Herbart's psychology of education. Thus, according to these criticisms, there should be more of teacher-pupil planning of objectives, learning activities to achieve the objectives, as well as evaluation procedures. How much the teacher should be involved in determining the curriculum, as compared to pupils involvement, has long been an issue in education. One may even conceive of removing decision-making from the teacher to the level of the state or nation. Thus, a highly centralized system of education might well be in the offing. At the ministry of education level then, goals of instruction would be chosen for implementation in the local classroom.

Toward the opposite end of the continuum, the student may choose from among alternatives developed by the teacher as to which objectives to achieve and which to omit. Or, a project method may be utilized in which the involved learner with teacher guidance plans what the former is to learn. Each student, as needs and interests dictate, would pursue a different project.

Bowyer[7] wrote:

> One of the most important and lasting contributions that Herbart made to pedagogical theory is his doctrine of interest. Interest, according to Herbart, is some inner tendency, and active power residing in the mind that urges the retention of a concept (an objective of thought) in the consciousness or a return of the concept of consciousness. The tendency is increased by the law of frequency and by the law of association. The primary task of the educator is to present the ideas constantly and consistently to the attention of the child. In this way, the teacher is able to control the experiences of the child, and to provide him with the sorts of insights that will mature his judgement.
>
> A recognition of the moral law is acted out by an exhibition of good judgement, decisiveness, warmth, and self restraint in all regards, and children should be educated to will the good so freely and so constantly that it becomes second nature. Since it is impossible to forsee what the choices and goals of the man will be, it depends upon the teacher to prepare the child with principles that should guide the normal man to good choices and with the abilities and qualifications that will enable the man to attain his goals. Therefore, it is highly essential for instruction to cover a wide range of subjects.

Herbart's psychology of sequential flexible steps to utilize in teaching students provided direction to the classroom teacher in emphasizing appropriate sequence in the curriculum. Since the teacher determines the order of experiences for students, a logical rather than a psychological curriculum is then in evidence. A psychological curriculum emphasizes students with teacher assistance selecting sequential goals to attain. The logical curriculum (programmed learning) versus the psychological (humanism) is still an issue in educational psychology.

Which subject matter would benefit students most is still open to debate. Certainly, diverse academic areas have their contributions to make in guiding students to achieve optimally.

One still is faced with the question of which knowledge has the most worth. Certainly, a study of history as well as literature by students, as advocated by Herbart, in terms of general education is important. Also salient and being advocated thoroughly presently is that students achieve well in science, mathematics, the fine arts, and physical education.

Johann Friedrich Herbart believed that developing the moral individual was the major objective in education. His predecessor at Konigsburg University, Immanuel Kant, had also placed much emphasis upon morality. In fact, in the Categorical Imperative, Kant stated that any person should act in a manner which emphasizes a universal rule, the Categorical Imperative was very similar to the Golden Rule in doing unto others as we would have them do to us. Thus, human beings are not to be utilized as means or stepping stones to an end. But, each person is an end in and of himself or herself. Morality then for Kant was the major goal of education. Herbart agreed with this objective.

To teacher would then need to provide correct ideas to students so that the latter could develop into being moral. With a mind like a blank sheet at birth and the environment (education) printing itself upon this original Tabula Rasa, quality teaching inclusive of moral ideas needs to be in evidence.

The develop the moral being, Herbart believed literature and history as two curriculum areas which would assist students achieving the major goal of education. In studying the noble lives of persons in literature as well as in history, selected ideas would be imprinted upon the minds of students when the teacher utilizes the steps of preparation, presentation, association, generalization, and use. Other curriculum areas, of course, were also important to the thinking of Herbart. However, literature and history, in particular, would help students achieve the goal of becoming ethical moral individuals.

The question always arises as to how any educator would discipline students. Certainly, one can think of physical punishment and methods of embrassment being used to correct unruly behaviour. However, when the teacher uses these two disciplinary methods, certain ideas and values are imprinted upon the minds of students. Thus, negative means of relating to other human beings would become a part of the student's acquired learnings. Rather, Herbart would advocate the instructor keep track of the time wasted by the student in class. Whatever time is not used profitably needs to be made up. Before the school day begins or after it ends could be suitable times for the learner to make up class time which had been utilized in an unprofitable way. A logical approach in disciplining students is then in evidence. The concept of logic in making up for lost time in the classroom reaches the level of consciousness in the student's apperceptive mass. A quality model then is experienced by learners and imprints itself upon the human mind.

Rene Descartes and Idealism

Descartes (1596-1650) believed that ideas predominate when knowledge is being acquired. He is known for his famous statement "I think therefore I am." Descartes attempted to doubt everything in order that he could arrive at certainty in knowledge. He found that the act of doubting indicated life was not an illusion, but reality and realness existed in the act of doubting. Descartes had to assume a benevolent being (God) who would not deceive and thus permit truth to occur, such as the act of doubting.

Rene Descartes, being a mathematician and having discovered differential calculus, emphasized an idealist idea centered philosophy based on mathematics. From selected axioms, Descartes deductively would arrive at truth through clear and distinct ideas. The individual would start with a statement of what is known as truth. From this statement which is clear and concise, the individual deductively would arrive at the next idea. This idea needs to be different from the first and still possess clarity. This sequence, a mathematical model, is followed until no further logically true ideas can be arrived at through thought that possess clarity as well as being distinct.

Descartes was very distrustful of sense perception. Reason and logic are better indicators of truth. Pertaining to the use of the senses, Descartes viewed a building from a distance and it appeared to be round. When getting near to the same building, it was shaped as a cube. Or, looking straight ahead, a road looks as if it is coming to an end. By going forward continually, the road is still there and continues in length.

Using mathematics as a model, one can reason from the general to the specific to obtain accurate information, according to Descartes.

Mind and matter were two different concepts. Each is made of a different substance. Descartes believed initially that mind and matter do not interact. The question then arose, "How do the arms and leg do what the mind desires or wishes?" More toward the end of his lifespan, Descartes believed the pineal gland, located at the base of the brain, was the source for connecting the mind (intellect) and the physical (body movements).

Ideas and rational thought are continually emphasized in Descartes thinking. Rene Descartes, a French philosopher, scientist, and mathematician, is considered by many to be the initiator of modern philosophy. Reason, rather than sense experience, was emphasized by Descartes. Descartes was educated at a Jesuit College and did much travelling. He received an adequate inheritance and could then devote his life to studying and writing. Mind, rather than body, was emphasized in the use of reason. Clear and distinct ideas could only come from reason and the use of the mind or intellect. Two types of ideas existed—clear ideas in which one idea could be differentiated from other ideas, and distinct ideas in which the inherent parts could be separated from other parts. Descartes believed that the salient task of philosophy was to take complex ideas and divide them into simpler component parts. This was tantamount to securing clear and distinct ideas.

The concept of God could only be due to this concept being placed into the mind of individuals by God. Perfection comes from God and a perfect Being places Himself into the minds of people. Since one can think of God, therefore the perfect Being exists in one's mind.

Rene Descartes believed that if he thought of God, the latter being existed. The perfect being which is then God, existed because noting with more perfection could be thought of. An ontological approach was then utilized by Descartes in attempting to prove God's existence.

Pertaining to innate ideas, Sahakian[8] wrote:

> The Cartesian *Cogito* which proves the existence of the soul beyond all doubt is one example of an innate idea, that is, an idea with which we are born, an idea which does not require sense experience as a basis for its validity. Mathematical axioms are self-evident and do not require factual proof; the same is true of innate ideas, axioms imbedded in the mind at birth. While ideas in general are images or copies of objectives of the external world created by sense perceptions, innate ideas have always been internal as part of the self, derived from one's own nature.
>
> They are eternal truths. The innate idea that one's soul exists does not have to be proved by experience external to one's own inner consciousness, and the same is true of other innate ideas. Descartes listed the following innate ideas: (1) God, who is as innate to me as my own soul; (2) ex nihilo nihil fit (out of nothing nothing comes), the principal that it is impossible that a thing can originate out of nothing, i.e., the principle that every effect must have a cause; (3) the principle of the impossibility that the same thing can both exist and not exist at one and the same time; (4) the idea that whatever is done can never be undone; and (5) the innate idea of the soul, namely, that when I think, I cannot be non-existent as long as I am thinking.

Descartes wanted to find certainty in ideas in the universe. He attempted to doubt all things in life. He even doubted that he was doubting. Descartes realized that thought was involved. Here Descartes' well known statement "I think, therefore I am" provided for him a basis for exact knowledge. The thinking person had to exist. Definite things could then be known. There, however was a further problem that Descartes identified. Could there be a deceiver who made it appear as if thinking as in evidence? Here, Descartes stressed the importance of a Divine Being who not permit deception to occur. Pertaining to an undeceiving God, Descartes[9] wrote the following in

Dualism and the Problem of Knowledge:

> Nevertheless I have long had fixed in my mind the belief that an all-powerful God existed by whom I have been created such as I am. But how do I know that He has not brought it to pass that there is no earth, no heaven, no extended body, no

magnitude, no place, and that nevertheless [I possess the perceptions of all these things and that] they seem to me to exist just exactly as I now see them? And, besides, as I sometimes imagine that others deceive themselves in the things which they think they know best, how do I know that I am not deceived every time that I add two and three, or count the sides of a square, or judge of things yet simpler, if anything simpler can be imagined? But possibly God has not desired that I should be thus deceived, for He is said to be supremely good. If however, it is contrary to his goodness to have made me such that I constantly deceive myself, it would also appear to be contrary to His goodness to permit me to be sometimes deceived, and nevertheless I cannot doubt that He does permit this.

Pertaining to the concept of God, Descartes believed since he could think of God therefore God exists. An ontological approach is involved in Descartes proving the existence of God. Anselm (1033-1109), Previously, had utilized a similar argument (ontological thinking) in proving God's existence. Anselm, Archbishop of Canterbury[10], stated:

And so Lord, do thou, who dost give understanding to faith, give me, so far as thou knowest it to be profitable, to understand that thou art as we believe; and that thou art that which we believe. And indeed, we believe that thou art a being than which nothing greater can be conceived. Or is there no such nature, since fool hath said in his heart, there is no God? (Psalms xiv. I). But, at any rate, this very foot when he hears of this being of which I speak—a being than which nothing greater can be conceived—understands what he hears, and what he understands is in his understanding, although he does not understand it to exist;

For, it is one thing for an object to be in the understanding, and another to understand that the object exists. When a painter first conceives of what he will afterwards perform, he has it in his understanding, but he does not yet understand it to be, because he has not yet performed it. But after he has made the painting, he both has it in his understanding, and he understands that it exists, because he has made it;

Hence, even the fool is convinced that something exists in the understanding, at least, than which nothing greater can be conceived. For, when he hears of this, he understands it. And whatever is understood, exists in the understanding. And assuredly that, than which nothing greater can be conceived,

> cannot exist in the understanding alone; then it can be conceived to exist in reality; which is greater;
>
> Therefore, if that, than which nothing greater can be conceived, exists in the understanding alone, the very being, than which nothing greater can be conceived, is one, than which a greater can be conceived. But obviously this is impossible. Hence, there is no doubt that there exists a being, than which nothing greater can be conceived, and it exists both in the understanding and in reality.

The ontological approach in proving the existence of God appears to lack harmony with Descartes mathematical model in thinking deductively from the general to the specific in a clear and distinct manner. However, Descartes emphasized the deductive clear/distinct philosophy in arriving at truth which ultimately placed God as a Being throughout space and time.

Throughout his writings, Descartes placed emphasis upon rational thinking, the intellect, or the mind to arrive at ultimate reality. The use of the sense of seeing, hearing, testing, smelling, and touching were not adequately accurate sources of information for Descartes. Descartes wanted certainty in knowledge which sense data could not provide. Mathematics as subject matter and as process could provide the accuracy in ultimate reality that Descartes craved.

Metaphysics in philosophy is an attempt to discern what is ultimately real. Truth with a capital T stresses that which can be discerned to be eternal and enduring. The senses are affected by the body and therefore cause erroneous thinking. A dualism then exists between mind and body. Descartes wrote as if mind and body are completely separate entities.

Descartes believed that the mind interpreted what was experienced by the senses. The mind was not controlled, nor a part of science, whereas the body is subject to the laws of science. The mind is more important than the body for securing accuracy of ideas. Rational thought with clear and distinct content makes for accuracy and certainty of ideas. Socrates in ancient Athens, before his execution, believed the mind survived the body. Descartes believed that the mind or soul could exist independently from the body. The mind or soul, being a substance which is independent from other substances, can then be completely detached from the body. According to Descartes, mind alone does the thinking.

In applying Descartes thinking to curriculum development, the following appear justifiable:

1. objectives of instruction should emphasize mental development. Mind is real and needs to be developed thoroughly through quality learning opportunities. Cognitive objectives would predominate in each curriculum area. Affective ends need emphasis in the curriculum to the degree that quality attitudes assist in intellectual development. Psychomotor objectives would receive little emphasis in Descartes' curriculum for students.

2. deductive methods should be utilized in teaching-learning situations. The teacher would explain meaningfully to students what is meant by clear ideas as well as what is meant by distinct ideas. Students with teacher guidance in each curriculum area would write what is known definitely in terms of subject matter and content. Deductively, the student then writes the next related idea that is different from the first and yet is meaningful and possesses clarity. The deductive sequence of ideas would follow until the student cannot meaningfully and with clarity write the next idea which is distinct.

3. students would strive for certainty of ideas following the mathematical model which emphasizes precision and exactness. Science, as a curriculum area, would also contain content which has specificity in content. Mathematics tends to be the language of science. Social studies does not possess the specific, precise knowledge that is true to science and mathematics. Neither does the literature and language domains possess this precision. As a further example, when issues are discussed pros and cons abound. Thus the quest for certainty is not always possible, by any means, in knowledge acquisition. Clarity of ideas and being able to distinguish subject matter discussed or in writing should always be a vital objective of instruction.

Charles Sanders Pierce, William James and Experimentalism

Pierce (1839-1914) was a rather early exponent of experimentalism. The consequences of an act or deed are of utmost importance. Ideas can be tested in a problematic situation to notice which does or does not work. Two ideas are both prized highly. Which is the better of the two? Each of the two is treated as a hypothesis. A hypothesis is tentative, not an absolute. Thus each of the two ideas is tested in a life-like situation. The consequences of each is noticed after testing. That which works is the better of the two ideas, as noticed by the consequences. Ideas have to be vital and relevant in order to be tested. If the consequences do not matter, the ideas have no worth.

Williman James (1842-1910) further advanced the philosophy of experimentalism. James spoke and wrote of the cash value of an idea. The cash value had to do with the consequences of each idea. That idea is best which, after being tested in a life-like situation, produces the best consequences. One looks at the results of testing each idea, not the intent therein. What is salient is quality results from ideas emphasized or to be stressed in an ongoing situation, deed, or act.

William James also placed importance on religious beliefs representing ideas that can be tested to determine the worth of each. Any religious belief can be tested in society to determine its worth or value. Religious beliefs make a difference in the person's life if there is a consequence which is positive.

Pierce and James emphasized the consequences of ideas, deeds, and acts rather than prizing subject matter for its own sake. Aristotle (384-322 BC) advocated knowledge being valuable intrinsically whether it be utilized in society or not. Pure contemplation or reflection then becomes salient.

Pierce and James stressed the concept of instrumentalism in acquiring content. Ideas are acquired as being instrumental to the solving of problems. Content is not prized intrinsically only, but it is useful and utilitarian. Thus content is valuable in the solving of problems. The worth of the knowledge is in its solving of problems, not for contemplative purposes. Testing of knowledge emphasizes cash worth. Knowledge that reveals the best results after testing has the most value. Intent of the person is not the most important item when individuals interact with others in society. Rather what happens to the results of an idea when it is utilized in society represents that which has value in practical situations. In philosophy, lengthy philosophical discussions have been held over the intent as reflected in Immanuel Kant's (1724-1804) thinking as compared to looking at the consequences of an idea being tested. The latter philosophy represents the thinking of Pierce and James.

Soren Kierkegaard and Existentialism

Kierkegaard (1813-1855) emphasized life as being subiective and filled with choices to be made. Each decision made, from among alternative possibilities, emphasizes subjectivity, not objectivity. Kierkegaard emphasized three broad levels that individuals may choose to go through in the decision-making arena. Step one represented the aesthetic. The aesthetic stage represents a lack of commitment. Here, the person engages in hedonist thinking in that pleasure becomes a major objective in life. Or, the Individual may choose to be an intellectually minded person, interested in the abstract, not in the doing of acts in society. Kierkegaard was greatly opposed to Georg Friedrich Hegel's philosophy of rationalism. Here, according to Kierkegaard the individual avoids existence and every day dilemmas in life. Rationalism stresses universals, abstractions, and ivory tower thinking. Rationalism removes the self from the awesome decisions that need to be made in life. Rationalism emphasizes an objective observer detached and removed from the burden of making individual choices and decisions. To be human is to be involved in the societal arena in the making of choices and decisions, accepting responsibilities for consequences of personal deeds and acts. In stage one, the hedonist lives for the present with no plans for the future. He/she does not commit the self to performing ethical deeds and acts. Being uncommitted in life makes for boredom. Empty feelings abound when boredom is in evidence.

Kierkegaard's second stage emphasizes ethics. In the ethical stage, authentic decision are made by the individual.

Commitments are made. Strong feelings, anxiety, and tension are inherent when choices are made. Being aware of death and one's final days makes for better deeds and acts by the involved person. To live a quality life, one must live as if the present day is the last one to be lived. One needs to know the self to make authentic choices which is a duty to fulfill.

Stage three emphasizes religion and religious beliefs. The religious stage stresses commitment and obedience to God. Faith is necessary to believe in God. Obedience to the will of God is a must in stage three. One first exists and then finds his/her essence. Suffering will come about due to the individual having moved to stage three, the religious stage. Being authentic in a transparent form before God emphasizes faith. A person must be conscious of the self to possess a will. A well developed will stresses an authentic self. Despair comes about if one is unauthentic. Faith overcomes despair.

Kierkegaard emphasized complete freedom for individuals in the making of choices. Choices to be made are subjective; other decisions could have been made instead of the original decision. Each person is finite; death is an ultimate to all individuals. One exists and then must find his/her essence or purposes in life. These purposes or goals are not given to anyone, but must be sought.

Existentialists believe that one. First of all, exists and is a person. The individual then tries to find his/her essence or purposes in life. Rene Descartes (1596-1650) stated that "I think, therefore I am." Existentialists believe the person is (exists) and then thinks (finds essences or purposes in life). It is up to the individual to establish purposes, goals, and reasons for existing. The individual then is responsible for choices made. Blame for consequences of decisions made can not be placed on others. The individual did the choosing and thus must accept the results of the choices. He/she makes the self. Each person must assume this responsibility.

Choices made are in an entirely open environment. Thus, it is awesome to think of the diverse possibilities involved in the making of decisions. Responsibilities for the decisions rest entirely upon the decision-maker. No other person can accept any responsibility. Existentialists can accept the theistic or atheistic position. Soren Kierkegaard (1813-1855), credited with developing existential philosophy was a theistic existentialist. Thus Kierkegaard believed that choosing and following God was a personal decision. He was opposed to a state religion where one is born into a specific religious group without personal choices made. Choosing God, rather than other goals in life, emphasized a choice made based on faith, rather than empiricism. With faith, certainty does not exist that an actual God exists. Faith is that which is hoped for. Evidence is not present when faith is emphasized. Kierkegaard personally made the leap to faith. The leap which Kierkegaard compared on jumping across the width of a stream of water emphasized uncertainty. Perhaps, the individual might not make the risky jump satisfactorily. An awesome responsibility exists in making these choices. Prior to the leap, two sequential previous stages of the individual's development have been.

1. living according to sense data in the here and the now.
2. emphasizing secular standards of conduct in this life.

Jean Paul Sartre (1905-1980), French atheistic existentialist emphasized the concept of *dread*. Individuals are born and then must make decisions. To make individual decisions is to be human. Dread is involved in making these choices. Choices are endless. One is condemned to be free since no God exists. If God did exist, a manipulator of human beings would be present. A superior being would tend to determine what each person is to do. With no God, complete freedom for individuals to make choices is in evidence. An awesome responsibility is inherent in making the choices.

Each person needs to view death as an ultimate in life. Humans struggle to do, act, and achieve. Yet, ultimately death comes to all. Even with facing one's death in time, purposes or reasons need to be found for living. The purposes must be found by each person and are not given to any individual. Anxiety is involved in each day of living. No person knows what the future will bring, but each needs to shape, through decision-making, his/her own destiny. Right beliefs and standards in an objective world do not exist. Rather, subjectivity is involved in the choosing arena.

Doubts; anxiety, and dread are a part of life. The individual needs to accept the idea of aloneness as being significant. The person is one among billions on the planet earth.

Perennialism and Thomism Harmonized

Perennialists advocate the Great Books concept in teaching students. The great ideas of the past are then emphasized in the curriculum. These ideas have stood the test of time and place as vital literature and content for all to study. A common body of knowledge is then available for all students. Recent literature is not a part of a perennialist's curriculum. Rather, one has to notice in time which writings survive diverse forms of scrutiny. From Plato (427-347 BC) to John Dewey's (1859-1952) writings, might well emphasize the Great Books concept in content to be taught to students. The content may be simplified when it is rewritten to the understanding level of students of different age and achievement levels. The original content, however, is to be emphasized.

St. Thomas Aquinas' (1229-1274) writing represents subject matter contained in the Great Books (perennialism) as well as the official theology of the Catholic church and Thomist education.

St. Thomas Aquinas emphasized reason and faith as representing the two highest levels of thought. Should the two (reason and faith) present a conflict, faith or revealed truth takes precedence. Thus, the intellectual soul is the highest facet of an individual's development. Objectives of instruction in Thomism then should emphasize faith and reason. Below the intellectual soul is the sensitive soul, according to St. Thomas Aquinas. The sensitive soul would achieve objectives dealing with the use of the five senser (observing, hearing and listening, testing, touching, and smelling). Psychomotor goals of instruction would emphasize locomotion which also is a part of the sensitive soul. Below the intellectual and sensitive soul is the vegetative soul. The vegetative soul pertains to nutrition (proper diet), growth, and reproduction.

Following the philosophy of Aristotle (384-322 BC), St. Thomas Aquinas emphasized four causes. A First Cause would be God. God caused the universe and all therein to happen. Aristotle called the First Cause the Prime Mover. Efficient is another cause. Someone has to keep the universe in operation sequentially after it was begun. According to St. Thomas Aquinas, God maintains and sequences the universe. Aristotle stressed the efficient cause as a worker who changes matter (material cause) to something else which has form. A third cause of St. Thomas Aquinas was formal. In the universe, order and harmony prevail. Anarchy and irregularities are not in evidence in the physical universe. For Aristotle, formal cause stressed the effect of material cause. Thus from matter (material cause such as wood), a chair (formal cause) can be made. From material cause to formal cause emphasizes a sequence of operations performed by the efficient cause. The final cause for Aristotle emphasized the use to be made of the formal cause. Many uses can be made of the formal cause. A bluerprint or plan of action is then in evidence. According to St. Thomas Aquinas, God has a plan for the universe and what is therein.

Thomism, Catholic Philosophy of Education, receives its name from St. Thomas Aquinas (1224-1273). St. Thomas Aquinas harmonized the writings of the Church Fathers with that of Aristotle (384-322 BC), philosopher of ancient Athens.

Thomism, as a philosophy of education, emphasizes a First Cause. The First Cause (God) created the world and the universe. Someone needed to start that which exists today, be it people, nature, and the natural environment. The starting was done and completed by the First Cause or God. An efficient cause created from matter (material cause) to that which is called formal cause. The universe then has form, structure, and design in what is called formal cause. From material cause (matter) to formal cause (form, structure, design) emphasizes an additional component part and that being a final cause. The final cause stresses the use that will be made of that which was designated as formal cause. The First Cause (God) has a purpose or plan for the universe and its inhabitants.

Human beings share with other forms of life, be it plant or animal the traits of growth, reproduction, and decay (death).

With animal life, human beings share the traits of sensation (using the senses) and locomotion (movement). Humans, however, alone can use practical reason (The Golden Mean). Thus, between two extremes, one takes a middle position, such as being too aggressive, versus being too timid. The highest form of reason is pure contemplation. Within the Catholic church, the individual meditates and contemplates eternal values and truths.

In harmonizing the Bible with Catholic education, a useful incident would pertain to Jesus "growing in wisdom, in stature, and in favour with God and man." In analysing this verse for Catholic education, wisdom would pertain to achieving goals in reading, writing, arithmetic, science, and social studies, as well as in the overall objective of developing skills to reason well. Stature emphasizes physical growth and development of students. A quality physical education programme is then needed. Being in favour with God stresses classes in Catholic religion. Being in favour with man emphasizes students achieving well socially and emotionally.

Priorities need to be set in education. The church and its beliefs would come first in Catholic education. The Catholic church and its philosophy of education sets it apart from other philosophies of education. Jacques Maritain[11] wrote the following in Thomism:

> Education directed toward wisdom, centered on the humanities, aiming to develop in people the capacity to think correctly and to enjoy truth and beauty, is education for freedom, or liberal education. Whatever his particular vocation may be, and whatever special training his vocation may require, every human being is entitled to receive such as properly human and humanistic education.
>
> Liberal education has restricted in the past to the children of the upper classes. This very fact reacted on the way in which it was itself conceived. Liberal education for all obliges us, I believe, to undertake a double reconsideration.
>
> In the first place, a serious recasting of the very concept of the humanities and the liberal arts has been made necessary by the development of human knowledge in modern centuries. The notion of the humanistic disciplines and the field of liberal arts must be enlarged so as to comprise physics and the natural

> sciences, the history of sciences, anthropology and the other human sciences, with the history of cultures and civilizations, even technology (in so far as the activity of the spirit is involved), and the history of manual work and the arts, both mechanical and fine arts.

Perennialism stresses that which endures in space and time. Perennialists look to the past for goals in education. Classical content which has remained salient in diverse geographical regions as well as in history is desired and believed to be, vital subject matter for student acquisition. Recently written content is not important. It may not survive as the decades and centuries progress. To be considered quality in ideas and content, time has to pass to know if the subject matter will survive.

Great ideas have survived in space and time. The late Robert Maynard Hutchins (1899-1978) and Mortimer Adler were/are advocates of university students studying the Great Books of the Western World. In the Great Books, the following writer's ideas are salient: Plato, Aristotle, St. Augustine, St. Thomas Aquinas, Peter Abelard, Rene Descartes, Gottfried Leibnitz, John Locke, Bishop Berkeley, Immanuel Kant, Georg Friedrich Hegel, Friedrich Wilhelm Nietszche, William James, and John Dewey, among others.

Perennialists believe strongly in a non-vocational curriculum. Rather, the liberal arts are to be emphasized as general education. Content in general education comes from the Great Books.

Perennialists look to the past for objectives of instruction. That which endures in ideas reveals worth and value. Ideas which do not last are forgotten and minimized, as well as forgotten. Inert ideas should not clutter the mind, nor should trivia. Perennialists believe the best way to determine subject matter which has value is to notice if it lasts and endures.

Perennialism emphasizes mental development as being the most important objective for student achievement. The mind is to reach out and grasp vital enduring ideas. Ideas represent the abstract facet of learning. Vocations, jobs, and occupations should be studied after adequate course work in The Great Books. Enduring ideas of the past should be shared by all as a common body of knowledge and thought. After the Great Books curriculum, individuals branch out into the diverse vocations that will be studied and trained for. Ultimately, a selection needs to be made of which role to play in the world of work, be it in the professions or other kinds of tasks.

Marxism as a Philosophy of Education

Karl Marx (1818-1883) has had considerable influence in education. It is very doubtful if nations claiming to adhere to Marxism actually adhered, even in degrees, to the philosophy of Karl Marx.

Marx emphasized a philosophy of collectivism. The individual is within a large group or collective. A major objective of education for the student is to work for the good of the collective, not for the self. Whatever is done in deed and act must harmonize with the goals of the group. The group or collective is more important than the individual. However, the individual achieves and is safeguarded within a group.

Karl Marx believed the worker to provide effort and be the productive force of goods and services produced in society. The worker is the dominant person in society. Workers represent the proletariat. Owners and managers tend to be parasites and live off of the worker's accomplishment in production and productivity. They represent the bourgeoisie. In Marx's surplus theory of labour, the worker gets only a small amount of the value received by owners and managers when selling goods and services to consumers. The profit of what was produced by workers goes to owners, managers, and corporation members. Workers then live poorly and receive few benefits from their labour. Workers have few, if any, rights in decision-making. They become alienated from their work. This is not the way it should be. Due to alienation, workers find joy in eating and procreating only.

Labour saving devices and technology make for increased unemployment and lower wages. Marx believed strongly in workers of the world uniting and joining together to size methods and means of production of good and services. Workers should do the decision-making of goods and services to be produced in society. They should benefit fully from their labour. Owners, mangers, and corporation members should not usurp the profit from goods and services produced by workers.

Marx believed in matter being more important than reason or the spirit. Georg Friedrich Hegel, a contemporary of Marx, believed reason or the rational part of the universe was predominate. Both Marx and Hegel believed in historical determinism with a triad of thesis, antithesis, and synthesis being in operation in the universe, Thesis indicated what was true presently. Antithesis emphasized the other end of the continuum from the thesis. A synthesis harmoized somewhat toward a middle ground position, from the thesis and the antithesis. For example, Marx believed that a society went through the following stages in sequence: primitive communism, slave, serf such as in the Middle Ages period of time, capitalism, socialism, and communism.

Marx believed that communism would be the dominant form of government and economic system resulting from the thesis, antithesis, and synthesis process.

Karl Marx stressed atheism as a set of beliefs. Marx emphasized that laws, regulations, rules, and government are already established prior to the worker's existence. The legislative, executive, and judical are already in place for the worker to abide by. Governmental policies, according to Marx, favour the entrepreneur in the business world. The entrepreneur then becomes increasingly wealthy. Laws favour the owner and manager in a capitalistic society to become wealthy. Rules in government work against the worker. The worker is reduced in income to bare subsistence and, perhaps, poverty. Workers should then unite to overthrow the yoke and bondage. They would then gain control of their own destiny.

Leaders in religion, such as Christianity, emphasized that workers accept their lot in life, even if it meant poverty and alienation. The workers' reward would then be in the hereafter in mansions of glory. To Marx, the hereafter concept was a fraud to keep workers in their place of working for low pay and living in poor situations so that entrepreneurs could reap wealth and riches. Poverty-ridden workers were told to wait for heaven when they would be rewarded for good deeds performed. Workers were to accept their low status in life as coming from God. Rewards for good living would come in heaven or at the completion of this life.

Pertaining to Marxism, Cohen[12] wrote:

> Karl Marx devoted his life to investigating the nature of man, to discovering the human essence, and in so doing he intended to achieve objective, scientific knowledge. His concepts and laws are not those of physics or even biology, his observational procedures are not the experiments of chemistry or the arboreta of botany, and as a scientist of human culture he may have found it of utmost difficulty to maintain an objective approach in the face of his own cultural background; but despite these differences Marx literally hoped to develop the science of society. Even this may have been subordinate to his simple goal of attaining the truth about man, for his initial observation, which leads to social science, is that man never exists in himself, he never lives as a true hermit. "Man" is the wrong word; we should speak of "men" and we should ground our every speculation about men on the concrete behaviour and relations of men as we find them. The most conspicuous feature of men and women is that they must be discussed in the plural; they are social by nature. The science of man will be the science of society.

SUMMARY

Each person has selected principles and ideals that guide human behaviour. Thus, diverse philosophies become important for study and implementation.

Realism follows a mathematics/science emphasis. Reality is based upon matter which is external to the observer. Matter is observable and can be known in whole or part as it truly is.

Idealism emphasized an idea centered approach in securing knowledge. One can know ideas only about what can be known through the senses. The world of ideas and reason abound to obtain concepts and generalizations.

Experimentalism stresses the world of experiences. One can know experiences only, of what the real world is like. Change is a key concept in life. With change, problems arise and need solutions.

Existentialism emphasizes a highly open-ended environment from which choices are made. To be human is to make authentic choices in an environment free from constraints. The consequences of each choice rest upon the chooser. Blame for wrong or undesired consequences cannot be laid upon others.

Perennialists believe in teaching enduring ideas in time and place. Goals in education come from the past in terms of vital ideas of great minds which have stood the test of time and place.

Thomism is a philosophy of education emphasized by the Catholic church. Beliefs in Catholicism are vital students attending Catholic parochial schools. However, growing in vital subject matter content, in physical development, and in social achievement are also salient.

Marxism stresses a collective philosophy of education. The worker, not owner or manager of industry and factories, becomes a person of major importance. Socially, useful labour is salient for all when individuals are old enough and able, including students in school.

Educators need to study diverse philosophical schools of thought. Each philosophy needs to be appraised in terms of merits or a lack thereof. Ultimately, those strands of thought need implementation that assist students to achieve more optimally.

REFERENCES

1. Bowyer, Carlton H. *Philosophical Perspectives for Education*. Glenview, IL: Scott, Foresman and Company, 1970, p. 159.
2. Locke, John. "Some Thoughts Concerning Education," *In the Works of John Locke*, volume X (London. Printed for W. Otridge and Son, et. al., 1812), pp. 6-7, 204-5.
3. Ulich, Robert, *History of Educational Thought*. New York: American Book Company, 1950, p. 208.
4. Wayper, C.L. *Political Thought*. New York: Philosophical Library Inc., 1954, p. 75.
5. Cubberley, Ellwood P. *The History of Education*. Cambridge, Massachusetts: Houghton Mifflin Company, 1948, pp. 759 and 760.
6. Ulich, Robert. *History of Educational Thought*. New York: American Book Company, 1950, pp. 277 and 278.

7. Bowyer, Carlton H. *Philosophical Perspectives for Education*. Glenview, IL: Scott, Foresman and Company, 1970, pp. 252 and 253.

8. Sahakian, William S. *History of Philosophy*. New York: Barnes and Noble Books, 1968, p. 136.

9. Descartes, Rane. *Dualism and the Problem of Knowledge*. New York: Cambridge University Press.

10. Chapters II through VIII of *Proslogium*, tr. by S.N. Deane, Open Court Publishing Company, 1903.

11. Maritain, Jacques. *Modern Philosophies and Education*. Chicago: The National Society for the Study of Education, 1955, pp. 77 and 78.

12. Cohen, Robert S. "*The Philosophy and Social Theory of Marxism,*" Modern Philosophies and Education. Chicago: The National Society for the Study of Education, 1955, pp. 117 and 178.

4

Recent Philosophers of Education

Valuable contributions to the philosophy of education have been made by selected Americans in the school curriculum arena. Their contributions lie in the areas of objectives, learning activities, and evaluation procedures.

William Heard Kilpatrick and the Project Method

Dr. Kilpatrick (1871-1964) was a strong disciple of John Dewey's (1859-1952) philosophy of experimentalism. And yet William Heard Kilpatrick's philosophy had unique facets. Kilpatrick emphasized the project method in teaching. The project method resembled projects that students had in the field of agriculture when taking agricultural classes in school. Thus dairy cattle, beef cattle, swine, and laying hens, among others, were examples of a project a student could have in the agricultural world. The student owned, took care of, and was responsible for his/her project. Accurate records were kept by the student of feed purchased and fed, straw secured, and other costs in taking care of the project. Students needed to plan, achieve the plan, and evaluate the quality of work done with each project.

Dr. Kilpatrick believed that the model of agricultural projects could be adaptable for students in the public schools.

Thus within a unit of study, the student with teacher guidance would identify a purpose. The purpose pertained to a goal to be achieved. Active involvement by the student is salient. With purpose, wholehearted involved in the project would be involved. Dr. Kilpatrick emphasized strongly that students were not to be passive recipients of knowledge. Thus listening to lectures, taking notes on each lecture, reading assigned pages of content, and discussing the related content were not recommended.

An actively involved student in learning then determines the project to be pursued. The project possesses the interests of the involved learner. Effort is then put forth to pursue and complete the project. Committee endeavours are also relevant. Social theory emphasizes that students learn to work together in completing one or more projects.

After the purpose has been chosen, the student of committee plans the purpose. Careful planning is necessary so that a quality project becomes and end result. The teacher guides, stimulates, and motivates students to develop as well as plan the purpose. After careful planning has occured for the project, implementation of the plans comes in sequence. Meticulous, creative work is necessary to develop the project. Finally, the completed project needs to be evaluated. Quality standards need to be utilized in the evaluation process.

During the time the project was conceived of as a purpose, as well as toward its completion, students engaged in relating reading, writing, listening, and oral communication activities. These learning activities were instrumental to the solving of a problem which was to develop and complete the project. An integrated curriculum was in evidence.

Dr. Kilpatrick emphasized that students learn to live in a democratic school setting where the latter needs to be involved in decision-making and choices. Students also need to realize and accept change as being ever present. A static world does not exist. No longer are students, if they have ever been, self-sufficient. Each is interdependent. Students interact within each other and in society. A changing world with better means of transportation and communication, continually being in the offing, has made for interdependence. Learning from books is not adequate. School and community should be integrated, not separate entities. Thus the community provides an excellent laboratory for objectives in the curriculum.

Dr. Kilpatrick believed that whoever is affected by a policy or rule should have a voice in its development. This is democracy. Students in school then should have a voice in determining the curriculum as well as standards of conduct. The student will be affected by these standards.

Unit Teaching and the Curriculum

Henry Clinton Morrison (1871-1945), late professor at the University of Chicago, emphasized unit teaching as a concept to organize instruction. A unit emphasizes relating subject matter areas into a whole. Isolation of content is then to be avoided.

Morrison advocated a definite method of instruction within the framework of unit teaching. A teacher then determines which vital facts, concepts, and generalization students are to acquire and learn. A pretest is given. The teacher then teaches to have students achieve selected subject matter content not mastered as a result of the pretest. After instruction, the teacher tests students over what had been taught. That which was not learned, as indicated by test results, is taught again until mastered by the student. Additional subject matter is continually brought into the teaching act as needed, followed by testing to notice student achievement. Teach, test, teach, and test was advocated as a methodology of teaching by Henry Clinton Morrison.

Morrison then attempts to have students perceive knowledge as being related within a unit of study. He believed that students should only be taught what was not known within the unit. To determine what has been known, tests were administered to be students. What has not been acquired, as revealed through testing, is retaught. Now subject matter is brought in for teaching as needed. The teacher determines *what* (the objectives) should be taught as well as the sequence or order of subject matter to be acquired by students. The teacher develops the tests to be utilized in measuring learner progress. Thus the objectives, learning activities, and evaluation techniques are determined by the teacher within the framework of unit teaching. Pertaining to Morrison's educational philosophy, Brameld[1] wrote:

> Morrison's theory is another interesting sample of the realist approach to curriculum building. Although he is himself impatient with formal philosophy, his writings contain many beliefs that seriously require philosophic inspection. He holds that the supreme purpose of education is "adjustment" interpreting the term, according to a central postulate of realism, as adjustment to "natural law"-to "conformity with the general trend of all evolution" and "to the conditions of civilized existence" Like many essentialists, Morrison never questions whether this trend and these conditions are generally satisfactory, simple implying that they are. Judd shares Morrison's governing beliefs and overall position with, however, some qualification.

Herman Horne (1874-1946) was a strong idealist in the educational arena. The soul and mind were the most salient factors of each human being to develop. Both were vital realities and needed adequate attention in teaching-learning situations. Horne strongly emphasized that importance is there, beyond what the senses can perceive. Thus, a reality beyond the natural world is in evidence.

Ultimate reality, for Dr. Horne, was the mind/soul. Beyond the physical world that human beings are acquainted with is the spiritual. Important knowledge comes through reason, rather than through the senses. Purpose or reasons for life are in evidence continually.

Dr. Herman Horne believed in his philosophy of idealism that the present life and the hereafter are both important. The hereafter, the unseen world, is needed due to a single life span for a person not being adequate in duration.

Human beings are much more important than animals. God created man in his own image and not as an animal. The finite being (humans) need to become more like the Infinite (God). Even though humans are finite, they are the crown or apex of creation.

Self-cultivation or developing the intellect is of utmost importance. The self needs to find himself/herself in serving others, rather than the self. Losing oneself to being a servant of humanity makes it so that the person finds values and goals in life.

An idealist needs to be a dreamer of ideas and speculate on God, the universe, and the liberal arts. Reason and imagination (creativity) are important to an idealist in developing the intellect.

A quality liberal arts curriculum is the heart of idealist thinking. Mathematics, the sciences, the social sciences (history and geography in particular), literature and languages, and the fine arts have important places in the liberal arts. The liberal arts are essential in developing the intellect.

School experiences cannot, by any means, always be interesting to students. Thus the will by the student is needed to master subject matter. The learner then must reach out and put forth much effort to learn. The will of the student needs to be involved in developing well intellectually.

Herman Horne believed in absolute truths. God or the Absolute emphasizes a definite curriculum of truths. Horne disagreed with the experimentalists in that the latter stressed continuous change being in evidence in the universe. With changes, knowledge does not remain stable, but is subject to much modification. Experimentalists also advocated that in the world of change, human beings make knowledge. John Dewey (1859-1952), as an experimentalist, believed the here and now being vital only, rather than an idealist's hereafter. Dewey did not believe one could have knowledge about a remote world (heaven) as idealists stress. He then advocated human beings should focus on the planet earth in identifying and solving problems therein. To Dewey, education represents growth and change. Horne stressed that growth is toward the Absolute or God.

Pertaining to Horne's philosophy of idealism, Pulliam[2] wrote:

> Another critic of Dewey who fits within the category of perennialism was Herman H. Horne (1874-1946). In his books *Idealism and Education* and *The Democratic Philosophy of Education,* Horne identified intelligence as a super human gift which links man with the absolute. Dewey's philosophy is naturalistic while Horne's is theistic. Truth for Horne is absolute and spelled with a capital "T," while for Dewey truth is merely a term for ideas which work in a given situation. Rejecting the view that education

is the reconstruction of experience, the idealist sees education as an understanding of the individual and social life patterns antecedent to present experience. Dewey tells us that education is growth or evaluation. Horne says that education is growth toward Truth and God.

John Dewey and Experimentalism

John Dewey (1859-1952) lived during a period of rapid changes. When he was born and even into the early 1900's, the automobile basically did not exist. When he died in 1952, manufactured automobiles, as a whole, were very dependable with hydraulic brakes, heaters, and even a few with air-conditioners. Electricity had its beginning in the early 1890's and was highly refined with its uses in 1952 with electric ranges, dishwashers, clothes washers, and driers. From zero automobiles in 1859 to more highways and interstates being built to take care of the large number of automobiles in use in the present scene. In 1859 horse drawn farm equipment was utilized to plow, harrow, disk, and seed the farm land. By 1952 farm tractors had electric lights, hydraulic brakes, and could pull a plow with four to five shears in plowing the land. Tremendous changes then occured from 1859 (year of birth) to 1952 (year of death of Dr. Dewey).

With these and many other changes, problems need identification and careful delineation in the school curriculum, as well as in society. Each problem is vital. Information acquired in school needs to be utilized to solve problems. Knowledge is not attained for its own sake, but is instrumental to the solving of identified problems. In society also, information is secured from a variety of reference sources, useful to solve each chosen problem.

From the data gathered, directly related to the problem, a hypothesis is developed. A hypothesis results for each identified problem. The hypothesis is tentative and subject to change through testing. Testing is done in a like-like situation. The results of the test may confirm or refute the hypothesis. Minor revisions of the original hypothesis may also be needed. Generally, change will occur rather continuously.

John Dewey believed that one could *experience* the real world only. One could not:

1. receive ideas only about the real world, as idealists emphasized;
2. know the world as it truly is and receive a replica thereof, as realists believed.

Since one can only experience reality and the real world posits problems, solutions need to be found to solve problem areas.

John Dewey strongly emphasized democratic living be it in school or in society. Democracy, as a way of life, stressed input from all in the making of decisions by which all would be influenced. Decisions made then should effect involved persons. Decision-makers will be affected by decisions made. This happens in the societal arena and needs to occur also in the school curriculum. Thus, students need to be actively involved in developing standards of conduct by which they will be governed. Student-teacher planning to develop and enforce standards of conduct is must in a democracy, according to Dewey. Ample input into school governance needs to come from those who will experience the consequence of the rules and regulations. Students are citizens presently in the school/societal arena. Education then is not a preparation for the future. Rather, students presently are citizens identifying and solving problems. The present school should not be separated from the future. Nor should school and society be separate entitites. What is vital in society in problem solving is also salient in the identification and solving of relevant problem areas in school. Interest in the problems identified makes for effort in determining solutions. Interest and effort are one, not separate concepts.

Experimentalists believe in the complete act of thought in the educational arena. The complete act of thought emphasizes:

1. careful statement of identified problems;
2. information secured to offer solutions to each problem;
3. hypothesis development;
4. tests emphasized for each hypothesis;

5. acceptance, modification, or refutance of the hypothesis. Pertaining to experimentalism, also called pragmatism.

Eichelberger[3] wrote:

> The relationship between knowledge and reality (truth) that is used by many researchers today is that of the pragmatist. John Dewey (1910) was a principle spokesman for this position, which states that all knowledge is produced by human beings and that we can never distinguish between knowledge and truth. In empirical research, this means that if something works in practice then it is true, or we can assume that it is true. A truth (knowledge) that is not supported by further empirical study will be modified or discarded.

William Chandler Bagley and Essentialism

Dr. Bagley (1874-1946) was the author of *The Essentialist Manifesto*. The *Manifesto* summarized Dr. Bagley's philosophy of education. Bagley believed that a body of knowledge exists and can be identified which all students should attain. A common set of objectives are then available for all students to attain. Dr. Bagley opposed an elective system of courses whereby each student could select, from among alternatives. He believed with an elective system of course, students lost out on the basics. These basics where essential for each and every student to acquire without exceptions. According to Begley, the role of the school is to prepare students for adult roles in society. To do this, educators need to identify carefully the basics or a core body of knowledge for all students to acquire.

In a world of change, Bagely felt the school could be a stabilizing institution with the identified basics in the school curriculum as objectives of instruction. Furthermore, he believed in curriculum areas which were exacting and not subjective in nature. For example, Dr. Bagley did not approve of the social studies as a curriculum area. The social studies lacked precision. Rather history and geography should be taught. History and geography have stood the test of time and were important already in Colonial American schools in the 1600's. History has its precise subject matter in names, dates, and places of salient events of the recorded past. Generalizations, carefully selected in history, can also be precise, accurate, and vital. Geography also has its specific content to teach students. Plains, plateaus, rivers, valleys islands, and peninsulas, among many other vital concepts, represent specific subject matter which needs to be taught to students. Numerous quality generalizations also need student acquisition in geography.

Arithmetic, science, spelling, and reading stress precise areas of content, not opinions or vague conclusions in the school curriculum. Interest in learning is important, but the will (effort) of the student need to be there. Bagley believed that the interest factor in learning, too frequently, is overdone. Rather the student needs to discipline the self in order to learn and achieve. Discipline in the classroom needs to be such that the teacher can teach well and students can learn much. Giving attention to the whim and desires of students, generally, is not warranted. Instead students need to attend and discipline the self, as well as obey the classroom teacher.

Bagley opposed the following:

1. lax discipline in the classroom;
2. the correlated and fused curriculum;
3. interests of students heavily emphasized;
4. continual modification of the school curriculum;
5. an activity centered curriculum as stressed by Dr. Dewey and Kilpatrick. Instead vital subject matter should be taught;
6. student-teacher planning of objectives learning activities, and evaluation techniques. Rather, a properly trained and educated teacher should make these decisions.

Pertaining to essentialism, Drake[4] wrote:

> Changes in secondary education have also come about because of the work of the essentialists. The essentialists have been so called because of their passion for finding and passing on to youth "the essentials" of the human race, and especially those things which are of practical use today. The method of finding these essentials has been that of a factual analysis of present-day social use. The influence of the essentialist has been more of a reform of education than a reform of society. Led by such men as William C. Bagley, Herman H. Horne, W.W. Charters, and

Charles H. Judd, the movement found wide acceptance among school administrators.

B.F. Skinner and Reinforcement Theory

Dr. Skinner (1904-1990) advocates connecting a stimulus (S) with a response (R) through reinforcing the response (R). Operant conditioning is then in evidence.

B.F. Skinner experimented with animals in developing his theory of reinforcement. Continuous reinforcement of desired responses makes for goal attainment. Thus, rewards such as grain is given to pigeons for forming the numeral "eight". Successive approximations, according to B.F. Skinner, emphasize each animal coming closer and closer to achieving the goal. Achieving an objective means moving in the direction of its attainment. This is possible due to rewards given continuously for each step of achievement toward goal attainment.

With rewards provided for achievement, more effort is put forth in learning and increased chances for correct responses are in the offing. Successive approximation emphasizes attaining more closely continuously to the desired behaviour. Dr. Skinner also stresses shaping of behaviour. With a clear objective in mind, the experimenter shapes or molds behaviour in a desired direction. Inherent in reinforcement theory is to shape behaviour toward a specific end. To form the numeral "eight", as a precise objectives, shaping or forming of behaviour is necessary. Awards (reinforcement) are needed to shape the pigeon's behaviour toward specific ends.

Rewards are provided for each small sequential step of learning. For a pigeon to achieve in forming the numeral "eight", grain needs to be given, pallatable to the pigeon for being successful in each and every tiny bit of goal attainment.

B.F. Skinner's operant conditioning principles have been widely applied to school classroom situations. The behaviourally stated objectives movement is one example. These objectives are highly precise. Either a student does or does not attain a specific end. The ends of instruction are salient according to B.F. Skinner. Skinner focuses upon the ends, not the means (learning activities). If students attain goals this is what is important. The learning activities are significant only to the degree that they assist and guide students to achieve objectives.

Skinner's operant conditioning principles also apply to rewards and prizes gives to students for achieving well. The rewards and prizes are announced to students prior to instruction. In this way, students know what to acquire as a result of instruction. With awards and prizes the response (R) is reinforced in S-R theory.

Skinner is a strong proponent of programmed learning. Programmed learning emphasizes a programmer determining precise objectives for student attainment, the involved learning activities, as well as appraisal procedures. A student achieves in small, sequential steps with continuous reinforcement. Pertaining to programmed learning, Harris and Sipay[5] wrote:

> Programmed materials are designed so that the user (1) encounters a series of small takes on which success is very likely; (2) is involved in the learning process through actively responding; and (3) receives immediate feedback as to the correctness of each response. In theory, programmed materials should greatly facilitate individualized instruction because they allow each student to work almost independently with material suitable for his or her needs, proceeding at a pace commensurate with ability and interest.

With the advent of Skinner, the measurement movement progressed rapidly. Student achievement was to be measured to notice learner progress. Only what can be observed and measured represents learning on the part of students. That which is interval had unobservable does not count as learned materials, skills, and attitudes. Exact measurement of students' achievement was advocated, not what represents opinions and fascinations.

Jerome Bruner and the Structure of Knowledge

Jerome Bruner professor from Harvard University advocates, as a philosophy of instruction, that students acquire structural ideas from academic disciplines. Burner believed that each academic discipline has a structure, or blue print, of knowledge, the structure of knowledge represents broad ideas, vital for student attainment, identified by academicians in their respective academic areas of speciality. Structural ideas pertain to the foundation of subject matter of an academic discipline. These major concepts and generalizations represent the core ideas of an academic discipline. Trivia is then weeded out.

The identified structural ideas by academicians are then made available to teachers. The structure of knowledge is then utilized as objectives for students to achieve. Inductive methods are utilized by the teacher to guide students to achieve the structural ideas. Students learn to utilize the same methods of inquiry as do academicians in their academic areas of speciality. A variety of materials, experiences, and activities are then available to guide students to achieve structural ideas inductively.

Bruner emphasized a definite sequence in teaching students. The teacher, first of all, needs to utilize manipulative materials. Manipulative materials stress the utilization of objectives and items in teaching. A hands-on approach in learning is emphasized here. The five senses are then utilized to acquire knowledge. Second in sequence, Bruner emphasized using iconic materials. With the iconic phase of instruction, perceptions by learners are one step removed from the manipulative or the concrete. In the iconic stage of learning, students experience those activities which assist in developing mental images. The iconic materials include video tapes, video-disks, films, filmstrips, slides, single-concept film loops, pictures, and study prints. Pictorial representation of the concrete are represented in the iconic materials on instruction.

In the third sequential stage of instruction, students experience the symbolic. Symbolic materials represent the abstract stage of learning. Reading of subject matter represents the symbolic stage of learning. Words read represent a code. The reader needs to decode the letters and words to determine meaning. Writing is a further example of the symbolic. Encoding is involved in writing. The writer uses a code (graphemes) to convey the information.

Joyce, Hersh, and McKibbin[6] wrote the following pertaining to Jerome Bruner's philosophy of education:

Since the publication of Jerome Bruner's influential book (1961) much emphasis has been placed on the organizing concepts within academic disciplines. Bruner's thesis is that within each discipline there is a network of ideas that contain the major relationship within the field. For example, sociologists use ideas like norms, sanctions, and roles to describe what has been learned about in small groups. Hence, if we are to follow Bruner's structural principle, we would build a course on small groups around these ideas. In mathematics, one would teach the fundamental operations (addition, subtraction, multiplication, division) in such a way that the ideas or principles that control those operations were revealed and used to organize the material. In science, biology courses would be organized around ideas like structure and function that unify the content, whereas units on machines would be held together with ideas like force, mechanical advantage, and so on.

Bruner's statement of the advantages of the structure's principle has been taken seriously by many of the leaders of the academic reform movement. Following Bruner's lead, curriculum developers in several areas are using the structural principle. For example, grammar and spelling courses are organizing around principles from linguistics. Even reading programmes are being developed using phonetics, linguistics, and semantics as the source of unifying ideas. Bruner sees four advantages in this approach:

1. The structural ideas provide a conceptual map of the field that aids memory. The learner, in a sense, has an organizing structure on which to hang incoming information;
2. The student who masters the structural ideas has a sense of control over the discipline that is not yielded by factual coverage alone;
3. Organizing concepts provide a basis for applying learning to practical situations. One has the ideas needed to manipulate information in problem-solving situations;
4. Organizing concepts are what the scholar uses. By teaching them to students, we enable them to think using the same tools that the advanced researcher employs. This will undoubtedly lead to more scholarly careers.

Jean Piaget and Developmental Psychology

Jean Piaget (1905-1980), Swiss developmental psychologist, found that children progress through diverse stages, from infancy on. What is taught (the objectives) and sequence in learning (subject matter taught) depends upon the present stage of development of each student.

Piaget's first identified stage of development is sensori-motor. The sensori-moter stage lasts from birth to two years for the infant. Here, the young child develops the utilization of the five senses—seeing, hearing, tasting, touching and smelling. Motor development results in better eye-hand coordination through the sensori-motor stage of development. Parents and day care centers should provide activities for sensori-motor pupils which

1. aid in developing the five senses. Concrete materials from the very basis of sensori-motor activities.
2. assist in promoting the use of gross muscles with materials that can be manipulated.
3. develop feelings of satisfaction and reward.

Piaget identified the second stage of development as being preoperational. The preoperational stage approximates the ages of from two to seven years of age. Here, the pupil perceives one variable only. Two equal lumps of clay can be held out to the preoperational child. The child sees one of the two lumps flattened. Now the preoperational child is asked "Which of the two lumps has more clay?" The preoperational child sees diameter only of the flattened lump having more clay as compared to the other lump. Or, two identical tumblers can be filled with water. A taller, thinner tumbler is placed beside the above named two tumblers. With the preoperational child observing, the teacher pours water from one of the two tumblers into the taller thinner tumbler. Which tumbler now has the most water inside of it? The preoperational child looking at one variable, the height of the tumbler, will say, "The taller tumbler." The child here is not looking at the second variable which is the diameter of the taller tumbler, the preoperational child perceives one variable only.

A third stage of child development is the concrete operations stage. Here, in his clinical research, Piaget noticed that students, ages seven through eleven, notice several variables at one time. Thus in giving definitions to vocabulary terms, several meanings are provided by learners. Concrete materials need to be utilized rather heavily, as was true of the sensori-motor and preoperational stages.

Stage four, Piaget labeled *formal operations.* Increased abstract thought is now possible for students without the use of concrete materials of instruction. Diverse variables are analyzed and discussed through the utilization of abstract methods of instruction.

Jean Piaget's stages of development differ from Jerome Bruner's hypothesis of instruction which is "Any subject matter can be taught in some honest intellectual form to any child at any stage of development." A stages philosophy of instruction is not in evidence in the hypothesis presented by Jerome Bruner. Dr. Bruner believes that materials (manipulative, iconic, and symbolic, in sequence) and methods of instruction (inductive learning) make the difference in terms of when selected subject matter is taught, rather that the stage of pupil maturation. Pertaining to Piaget's thinking and research, Thiessen, Wild, Paige, and Baum[7] wrote:

> One theorist who supports the use of models for teaching is Jean Piaget. In his study of the intellectual growth of children he describes four sequential stages. Children proceed through these stages at different rates and different ages, depending on the influence of many factors. In addition to experiences, both intellectual and psychological, Piaget cites physiological maturation and social environment as factors that affect development at various stages. Also, an individual may be in more than one developmental stage at the same time. This person may be ready to think abstractly about number but still be in the concrete stage for geometric concepts.
>
> Children in the early elementary grades are most likely to be in Piaget's preoperational stage. They need to manipulate objects and observe the results of their actions on the objects. For example, children at the beginning of this stage lack conservation of number. If they count out two sets of ten objects in one-to-one correspondence, they will probably decide that there are the same number of objects in each set, However, if the objects in one set are spread out, the children may conclude that this set contains more objects than the other set. Experiences in counting, and

rearranging objects and observing their actions on the objects will help children become conservers of number.

As preoperational children mature intellectually, psychologically, physiologically, and socially, they will proceed gradually into the concrete operational stage. Children in this stage still need to manipulate concrete objects, particularly when a new topic is being introduced. However, if the object is not available, they can sometimes imagine pictures of that object. For example, instead of manipulating blocks, they form pictures of blocks in their minds and mentally manipulate the pictures. Since these pictures are based on previous experiences, a number of activities using models must be provided to help the children build these images.

Piaget's fourth stage is formal operations. At this stage individuals are able to think abstractly. They are not dependent on real or imagined objects. They are able to consider possible ideas as well as real and representational ones. They are able to formulate hypotheses and draw logical conclusions from them. Many children do not reach this stage during their elementary school years.

SUMMARY

Numerous recent philosophers and psychologists with their thinking were discussed. These include the following:

1. William Heard Kilpatrick and the project method;
2. Henry Clinton Morrison and unit teaching;
3. Herman Horne and idealism in the curriculum;
4. John Dewey and experimentalism;
5. William Chandler Bagley and essentialism;
6. Jerome Bruner and the structure of knowledge;
8. Jean Piaget and developmental psychology.

Each of the above has selected basic assumptions, knowledge, beliefs, and values which provide direction for the teacher in teaching students. Diverse philosophies have specific and general beliefs which give impetus to the teaching-learning situation. Teacher, principals, and supervisors need to study and analyze each philosophy in depth. Based on the study, decisions can be made as to which Philosophy/philosophies would best provide for each learner in the classroom. This should assist each student to achieve more optimally.

REFERENCES

1. Brameld, Theodore., *Philosophies of Education in Cultural Perspective.* New York: Holt, Rinegart and Winston, 1955, p. 251.

2. Pulliam, John D., *History of Education in America.* Columbus, Ohio: Merrill Publishing Company, 1987, p. 175.

3. Eichelberger, Tony R., *Disciplined Inquiry: Understanding and Doing Educational Research.* White Plains, New York: Longman Inc., 1989, p. 11.

4. Drake, William F., *The American in Transition.*, Englewood Cliffs, New Jersey: Prentice Hall, 1955, p. 465.

5. Harris, Albert J. and Sipay, Edward, R., *How to Increase Reading Ability.*, White Plains, New York: Longman Inc, 1985, p. 71.

6. Joyce, Bruce R., Hersh, Richard H., and McKibbin, Michael., *The Structure of School Improvement,* New York: Longman Inc., 1983, pp. 257-258.

7. Thiessen, Diane, Wild Magaret, Paige, Donald D., and Baum, Diane L. *Elementary Mathematical Methods.*, New York: Macmillan Publishing Company, 1989, pp. 71-72.

5

Philosophy of Measurement and Evaluation

There are numerous means available to ascertain pupil achievement. Diverse specialists in the measurement and evaluation arena list, among others, the following approaches:

1. criterion reference tests;
2. norm referenced (standardized) tests;
3. personality tests;
4. teacher observation;
5. teacher written test items, i.e. true-false, completion, matching, essay, and multiple choice;
6. anecdotal records;
7. sociograms;
8. portfolios;
9. interest inventories;
10. file of completed projects of students, such as written work, to make comparisons of earlier versus more recent endeavours to notice progress.

Each approach utilized to appraise student achievement has an attached philosophy.

The Testing Movement

When testing movements are stressed, a definite philosophy is involved. With testing of student achievement, the following assumptions are in evidence:

1. Something exists or *is* for testing to take place. If nothing existed, measurement is not possible;
2. With the existence of something, quantification is possible. One can then measure whatever *is* in some quality.

The testing and measurement movement has been in evidence for sometime. During World War I, tests were developed and used to separate men who would be officers as compared to those being followers. Detroit, Michigan used an X, Y, Z plan of grouping pupils for instruction in 1920. Pupils were then placed into one of three intelligence quotient levels for classroom instruction.

E.L. Thorndike (1874-1949) believed that testing and measuring of students' achievement could take place in any curriculum or academic area. He and his followers wrote and used arithmetic, handwriting, spelling, reading, and writing tests. These, along with intelligence quotient (IQ) tests, were written. The testing and measurement movement became increasingly fashionable with standardized test in academic achievement, personality development, interest inventories, vocational inventories, aptitude, mental maturity, along with others. Pertaining to E.L. Thorndike, Thayer[1] wrote:

> The early years of the twentieth century were conspicuous in the applications of science to all phase of business and industry. It was applied not merely to the invention of new products and processes but to the details of organization and management designed to promote economy and efficiency. Experts trained in "scientific management" studied carefully the performances of workers on the job with results so fruitful in economy and efficiency that many can to be seen in "job analysis" possibilities of application not only to vocational education but to the reform of other aspects of education as well. All that was needed, it seemed, was to identify the specific outcomes by insuring that pupils engage in the activities certain to eventuate in the proper habits and skills, information, attitudes, ideals, and the like.

> The new emphasis in the selection and organization of subject matter received definite formulation in 1918 with the report of the National Commission on the Reorganization of Secondary Education. This Commission stated the areas of concern, or the functions of the secondary school, in the form of Cardinal Principles. Its preliminary statement read: "In order to determine the main objectives that should guide education in a democracy, it is necessary to analyze the activities of the individual. Normally he is a member of a family, of a vocational group, and of various civic groups, and by virtue of these relationships he is called upon to engage in activities that enrich family life. To render important vocational services to his fellows, and to promote the common welfare."

Measurement and assessment has developed valuable concepts and generalizations. Sophisticated terms such as the following are utilized to determine validity of tests; content or face, predictive, concurrent, and construct. The following terms were generated to ascertain reliability: test-retest, split-half, alternative forms, as well as test-retest combined with alternative forms.

Standardized academic achievement tests, also called norm referenced, have been utilized much over the past four decades to notice student achievement. Intelligence quotient (IQ) standardized tests have an equally long history of utilization.

During the 1980's the accountability movement was emphasized by educators, as well as the lay public. Measurable results were then wanted from each public school student. Student achievement in the academic areas were revealed through testing. Subjective statements of learner achievement, were not acceptable in the accountability movement. Some public schools used standardized tests to notice academic achievement, provided in numerical terms. Many states and school districts within a state determined precise, measurably stated objectives for students to attain. These objectives were available to teachers prior to instruction in any academic discipline. Predetermined objectives were then available for learner achievement. The teacher's task was to select learning opportunities which guided students to achieve the precise, measurably stated objectives. After instruction, a student either had or had not achieved any given objective.

Criterion referenced test (CRT's) are written to align with the precise measurably stated objectives, emphasized in teaching-learning situations. Thus the concept of content or face validity has been emphasized in testing to notice student achievement. Norm referenced, standardized tests do not emphasize the utilization of predetermined objectives in teaching. With the accountability movement, diverse states have emphasized using criterion referenced tests to notice student progress. The criterion referenced tests may be written on the state level and be mandated for all students to take at different grade levels as learners move through sequential years of schooling. Criterion referenced tests to harmonize with measurably stated objectives may also be written on the district level, generally referred to as instructional management systems.

The testing and measurement movement is one philosophy of evaluation to ascertain student progress. Objective results only are used within the criterion referenced tests. Subjectivity is eliminated in appraising student achievement, according to advocates of the testing and measurement movement. Thus evaluation procedures such as the following tend not to be recommended: teacher observation, essay test items, anecdotal records, sociograms, and portfolios of students' completed work products.

Realism as a philosophy of education is reflected with the testing and measurement movement. Realists state that individuals can know the real world in whole or in part as it truly is. Each measurably stated objective achieved indicates certainty if students have been successful in learning. Each measurably stated objective pertains to a part of the real world.

Self Evaluation by Students

Existentialists stress students being heavily involved with teacher guidance in the selection of objectives, learning activities, and evaluation procedures. Thus, students are to make choices, from among alternatives. To be human is to make decisions. The student should not permit others to make decisions for the self.

Knowledge to an existentialist is subjective. Values clarification, literature, history, religion, art, and music become major academic areas to pursue in the curriculum. A learning centers philosophy may illustrate an existentialist curriculum. With learning centers, more tasks are available than what any student can complete. Thus the student may omit tasks that lack perceived interest, purpose, and meaning. Time on task is salient. The teacher becomes a stimulator and guide rather than a lecturer and dispenser of information.

Since students, together with the teacher, are actively involved in selecting objectives, learning opportunities, and appraisal procedures, existentialist philosophy places heavy emphasis upon students appraising the self to determine achievement and progress. This can be emphasized in diverse ways, including the following:

1. asking students what they would do differently when having completed an art project;
2. having students brainstorm different settings possible for a literature selection;
3. stressing that students develop their own collection of poetry, after readiness activities have been pursued;
4. encouraging students to think of alternate ways of behaviour than that exhibited by a person or nation, in historical units of study;
5. stimulating interested learners to set words in their written poetry to music.

Truth is in the eye of the beholder, according to existentialists. What is regarded as being *true* in evaluation results must come from the learner. The learner appraises the self with minimum teacher help.

A contract system may also be utilized to determine if goals have been attained by students. Thus the student determines *which* tasks need to be completed and written in the contract. The learner may also state n the contract which appraisal procedures will be utilized to determine progress. The teacher motivates and encourages students to list quality activities and experiences, as well as evaluation procedures, within the contract. The due date is placed on the contract and signed by both student and the teacher. Committee endeavours can be written in the contract if this is wanted by the involved students.

An individualized reading programme in any curriculum area further emphasizes tenets of existentialism. An adequate number of titles and reading levels of books needs to be in the offing for students to select from. The learner is the chooser of sequential library books to read. After a library book has been read, the student needs to select the procedure of evaluation, for the teacher to notice learner achievement. Open-endedness is involved when the student selects the means of appraisal, be it discussing the content with the teacher, drawing one or more sequential pictures to reveal knowledge acquired, pantomime one or more scenes, doing a creative dramatics presentation, and/or write a related play with salient parts or roles.

Self evaluation emphasizes existential tenets. The learner is in a central position to determine ways of self evaluation to indicate understandings (facts, concepts, and generalizations) as well as skills and attitudes achieved. Pertaining to existentialism, Ozman and Craver[2] wrote:

> It is interesting that most existentialist and phenomenological philosophers have had lengthy and rigorous educations. Most of them taught at one time or another, usually in a university setting. They have been concerned primarily with the humanities and have written extensively in the genre. Through the humanities the existentialists have tried to awaken modern individuals to the dangers of being swallowed up by the megalopolis and runaway technology. This seems to have taken place because the humanities contain greater potential for introspection and the development of self-meaning than other studies.
>
> The humanities loom large in an existentialist curriculum because they deal with the essential aspects of human existence such as the happy, the absurdities as well as meaning. In short, existentialists want to see humankind in its totality—the perverted as well as the exalted, the mundane as well as the glorious, the despairing as well as the hopeful, and they feel that the humanities and the arts do this better than the sciences. Existentialists, however, do not have any definite rules about what should comprise the curriculum. They believe that the student-in-situation making a choice should be the deciding factor.
>
> Although existential phenomenologists have been interested in understanding the lived experience of the learner than in the

specific content of things to be learned, some of them have given attention to curriculum organization and content. The tendency, however, is to view curriculum from the standpoint of the learner rather than as a collection of discrete subjects.

Idealism and the Evaluation Process

Idealists emphasize an idea centered curriculum. Vital subject matter then needs to be emphasized in teaching-learning situations. Higher levels of cognition need to be emphasized in teaching such as students engaging in critical thinking, in developing concepts, and in acquiring generalizations. Mental development is salient to idealists. Knowledge objectives become more significant for student achievement as compared to attitudinal goals. Skills are salient for students in order to develop higher levels of cognition.

Abstract ideas are more important for learners to acquire as compared to the semi-concrete and the abstract. The concrete and semi-concrete learning opportunities are important to the degree that students are better able to achieve in the abstract.

To appraise student achievement in knowledge and skills goals, vital and lively discussions led by the teacher assist students to reveal academic subject matter acquired. The idealist teacher needs to be an academically inclined person who stimulates students to participate actively in these discussions. All students need to participate so that increased knowledge and skills are developed. The student then moves away from the finite or limited to the Infinite (unlimited).

Evaluation procedures should indicate to the teacher how well students are achieving in the abstract. Quality, well written essay tests assist the students to reveal knowledge, critical thinking, concept development, and acquisition of generalizations.

The idealist teacher needs to avoid students attaining at a low-level of cognition such as achieving facts largely or solely. Rather, the teacher needs to appraise concept development and achievement of generalizations by students. Mental development occurs when students are challenged to study vital subject matter in a liberal arts curriculum. The subject matter is non-vocational and is needed by all students to be considered as educated individuals.

Students then need to be appraised in terms of growth in the utilization of the mind. Teachers need to observe in discussions and in essay tests, among other procedures, if learners are moving away from the finite to the Infinite being. The abstract, the mind, and subject matter are vital concepts to consider in the instructional arena. Pertaining to idealism, Wahlquist[3] wrote:

> All philosophic schools are concerned with the nature of reality. Reality, in the philosophic sense, is the property of being real, of really existing, despite appearances, as opposed to the imaginary, the factitious, or the merely apparent. The idealist holds that reality, i.e., the final stuff, is of the nature of Mind. He believes that back of and beyond the visible physical world is the real world of mind or spirit. From this viewpoint, the apparent self-sufficiency of nature is an illusion; nature depends upon something else, call it mind, spirit, or idea. The real substance of things, the ultimate being which explains all other beings, is thought to be more than physical or material. In theological circles this ultimate being is personified as God.
>
> The idealist says, in effect, if one seeks for elemental things, he will not find them in matter, motion, or force, but in reason, intelligence, personality, and values. Moreover, these realities have a cosmical significance; they are essences that bring order and unity into the universe. Hence, physical bodies and forces are secondary, being, as it were, externalizations or manifestations of the mind. Also, these ultimates do not depend upon human beings for their significance; they have an independent existence.

Experimentalism and Evaluation

Experimentalists advocate students with teacher guidance identifying and solving problems. These problems should be life-like and not fictitious. Thus human beings need to interact with each other to find solutions to identified problems. Artificial and textbook given problems do not emphasize problem solving. Problems chosen must be present in society. The school curriculum and the curriculum of life in society must become one, not separate entities.

Experience is all that one can know, not things as the really are in and of themselves (realism), nor does one receive ideas only of the natural/social environment, as idealism advocates.

Situations in life change continuously and thus problems arise continually. A changeless society is definitely not in evidence. Tomorrow will be different, in degrees, as compared to the present. Students need to accept change and realize that problems are an end result. Students also need to realize that the curriculum of life should provide objectives in teaching-learning situations within the school.

How then should the experimentalist teacher appraise student progress?

1. Noticing how effectively the learner identifies relevant problems.
2. Determining the quality of reference sources found by the student in gathering data to solve problems.
3. Assessing the worthiness of hypotheses developed.
4. Appraising the quality of hypotheses testing.
5. Being able to revise the tested hypothesis if needed.

A hands on approach to learning is emphasized in problem solving. Teacher observation is needed to appraise the quality of problem solving as revealed by students in an experimentalist philosophy of education.

Pertaining to John Dewey and experimentalism, Good and Teller[4] wrote:

> Dewey held that we think when when we must, and that thinking originates in a perplexity, and obstacle, or a doubt. Some have regarded this as a great discovery but it is in fact only a truism. If thinking is defined as the effort to find the answer to a problem or to resolve a perplexity, then, naturally, it cannot occur except in the presence of some difficulty. Like other truisms, however, this one is worth stating. It says that situations can be set up to stimulate thinking.
>
> The sources and varied nature of pupils' problems are themselves problems that closely concern the teacher. Children are active by nature, "spilling over with activities," and from these practical concerns many problems arise. Getting out of his playpen is for the small child a problem that is about on par with the problem of the cat in a cage. Rousseau and Froebel suggested many children's activities that involve problems, but they did not, like

Dewey, consider the detailed ways in which the problems are solved by children. Dewey suggests a few somewhat more intellectual but still simple problems. From How We Think everyone will remember the cases of the ferryboat with a white pole projecting from the front of the pilothouse, the soapy tumblers, and the problem in transportation.

Such examples are altogether appropriate as types of work for children; but may lead the students to the notion that problems usually or always arise from external conditions. This is not true. Philosophers including Dewey have often gone out in search of problems because they enjoyed thinking. Problems do not always arise from circumstances nor do they have to be assigned by a teacher. It is a fact of history that science has been created largely by pure scientists—Galileo, Newton, Faraday, Darwin, and a host of others—who went out to look for problems and investigated them for the love of it.

Perennialism and Evaluation

Perennialists look to the past for vital objectives in the present day curriculum. That which has endured in time and place is vital for students to study. Thus, the great ideas of thinkers in the past need emphasis in terms of quality objectives, learning opportunities, and appraisal procedures. Ideas need to survive in terms of time and place to become vital for students to acquire. Recent writings may not endure and thus became irrelevant as time passes by.

Mental development is a major goal for student acquisition when securing ideas, directly or simplified, from the Great Books, history and literature.

With stimulating discussions from content read by students pertaining to the classics, the teacher may evaluate:

1. how well learners attached meaning to the salient content;
2. how effectively ideas were organized sequentially by students;
3. how subject matter is being related when contrasting the ideas of great thinkers;
4. how thoroughly the ideas of the Great Books, history, and literature are being related;

5. how abilities are being increased to secure content by reading.

The teacher might also assess pupil progress in writing to reveal achievement in reading the classics. Thus, the teacher might notice the quality of paragraphs written, sequence in paragraph writing, higher levels of cognition emphasized in the completed product, as well as vital generalizations and concepts acquired by learners from the classics.

Evaluation procedures need to reflect upon students understanding content from the classics, having ideas acquired in an appropriate order, being able to analyze and synthesize content from the Great Books, attaining subject matter in greater depth, as well as appreciating salient ideas which have endured in time and space.

The Great Books in teaching and learning need to stress general education for all students. A common core of knowledge, skills, and appreciations should be an end result. Students need to be able to communicate well with others, when the classics are stressed in the curriculum. Vocational training and interests can come at a later time, generally after the baccalaureate degree has been obtained. General education, however, must come first be it on the elementary, secondary, or under-graduate levels of instruction. Vocational training emphasizes education for a specific career, job, or vocation. General education advocates that which all students need in terms of subject matter, abilities and attitudes to become quality citizens. The great ideas of the past whose concepts and generalizations have survived are the best bet for quality general education, according to perennialism. Pertaining to perennialism, Hutchins[5] wrote:

> But it seems to me clearer to say that, though it may be a system of training, or instruction, or adaptation, or meeting immediate needs, it is not a system of education. It seems clear to say that the purpose of education is to improve men. Any system that tries to make them bad is not education, but something else. If, for example, democracy is the best form of society, a system that adapts the young to it will be an educational system. If despotism is a bad form of society, a system that adapts the young to it will not be an educational system, and the better it succeeds in adapting them the less education it will be.

> Every man has a function as a man. The function of a citizen or a subject may vary from society to society, and the system of training, or adaptation, or instruction, or meting immediate needs may vary with it. But the function of a man as a man is the same in every age and every society, since it results from his nature as a man. The aim of an educational system can exist: it is to improve man as man.
>
> If we are going to talk about improving men and societies, we have to believe that there is some difference between good and bad. This difference must not be, as the positivists think it is, merely conventional. We cannot tell this difference by any examination of the effectiveness of a given programme as the pragmatists propose; the time required to estimate these effects is usually too long and the complexity of society is always too great for us to say that the consequences of a given programmes are altogether clear. We cannot discover the difference between good and bad by going into the laboratory, for men are not laboratory animals. If we believe that there is no truth, there is no knowledge, and there are no values except those which are validated by laboratory experiment, we cannot talk about the improvement of men and societies, for we have no standard of judging anything that takes place among men or in societies.

SUMMARY

Approaches utilized to appraise student progress depend upon the philosophy of education involved. Each specific philosophy has uniqueness attached in determining that which learners have acquired.

The testing and measurement movement stress the utilization of predetermined objectives written in measurable terms. The objectives are written prior to instruction of learners. With appropriate learning opportunities, either a student does or does not achieve one or more precise objectives. Measuring student progress against the stated objectives emphasizes the concept of criterion referenced testing (CRT).

The testing and measurement movement also advocates using norm referenced tests (NRT). Students are spread out on a continuum from highest to lowest based on test scores. Predetermined objectives tend not to exist when utilizing norm referenced tests to measure student achievement. Norm referenced tests spread students' results in terms of test scores much more so than criterion referenced testing. Students attempt to attain predetermined objectives with CRTs. The measurably stated objectives represent absolute standards. A high number of students might well achieve the measurably stated objectives, as the teacher usually intends.

Self evaluation by the student is an opposite approach to appraisal of learner progress as contrasted with the testing and measurement movement. With self evaluation, the responsibility rests with the learner himself/herself to acknowledge strengths, weaknesses, and modifications to attain at a higher level. Learners when evaluating the self need to perceive the processes and products completed from the frame of reference of personal improvement. Truth, in results from evaluation, may well reside within the student. Subjectively in results is to be expected, since open-ended criteria are utilized to appraise progress. The tendency here will be not to utilize objective tests to ascertain progress. With self-evaluation, the student might well perceive increased purpose in assessing the self. The teacher is a stimulator and initiator when guiding the self-evaluation process.

Idealism advocates students achieving well in mental development. Mental maturity here is prized more highly as compared to the effective and psychomotor domains of objectives. The affective dimension is salient to the point that learners attain well academically and intellectually. Students attaining vital concepts and generalizations is of utmost importance to an idealist. To appraise learner progress effectively, the teacher must evaluate student growth in achieving worthwhile subject matter content, consisting of vital broad ideas. Use of discussions and essay tests, in particular, assist the idealist teacher to determine student acquisition of subject matter.

Experimentalists depend upon teacher observation, basically, to evaluate student progress. The experimentalist teacher evaluates students in life-like situations to select and solve problems. Information needs to be gained by students to secure relevant answers to questions. Hypotheses, tentative in nature, attempt to provide answers to identified problems. Since each hypothesis is to be tested within a social context, modifications or revisions may need to be made.

Perennialism is a philosophy of conservation, rejecting a continually changing environment as identified and defined by experimentalists. The great ideas of relevant thinkers of the past provide subject matter content. The abstract and academic are to be preferred to the concrete and the practical. Transitory ideas from the past have no place in a perennialist's curriculum. Rather, content must remain salient, vital, and significant as the decades and centuries transpire. Endurance in time and in diverse geographical regions stresses that which is classic. The classics emphasis emphasize the liberal arts and general education for all. Preparing for jobs, careers, and the professions, as educational courses, have no place in a curriculum of perennialism. Vocational needs are not to be emphasized on the elementary, high school, or baccalaureate degree level, but on graduate levels of study which should prepare the student for a niche in the world of work. Prior to that time, however, common learnings should be acquired by students in the form of a liberal arts education.

Liberal education, consisting of the non-vocational, needs to emphasize as objectives of instruction the development of the mind to become mature mentally so that the great ideas of the past may be understood and accepted. Meaning must be attached to these great ideas. The Great Books provide an intellectual system of subject matter to be provided students. The content needs to be challenging intellectually and provide for retention of major concepts and generalizations.

REFERENCES

1. Thayer, V.T., *Formative Ideas in American Education*. New York: Dodd, Mead and Company, Inc., 1970, p. 224.
2. Ozman, Howard A. and Craver, Samuel M., *Philosophical Foundations of Education*. Columbus, Ohio: Merrill Publishing Company, 1990, p. 257.
3. Wahlquist, John T., Ph.D., *The Philosophy of American Education*. New York: Ronald Press Company, 1942, pp. 46 and 47.
4. Good, Harry G. and Teller, James D., *A History of American Education*. Third Edition. New York: The Macmillan Company, 1973, p. 372.
5. Chapter IV "The Basis of Education" from *The Conflict in Education*. By Robert M. Hutchins. Copyright 1953 by Harper and Row, Publishers, Incorporated, p. 351.

6

Issues in Education

Educators need to be thoroughly familiar in analyzing issues and trends in education. Each issue and trend needs to be appraised critically. A synthesis might be an end result in the curriculum.

Outcomes Based Curricula

An issue of relevance is to analyze an outcome based curriculum for students. Behaviourally stated objectives provide specific criteria as to what students should learn in any curriculum area. The objectives are stated to students prior to each lesson. After instruction, the teacher may determine if a pupil has or has not achieved each sequential objective. Either a student has/has not attained any stated objective. Criterion referenced tests are utilized to measure if students have been successful in goal attainment. The tests are aligned with the behaviourally stated objectives to emphasize validity. If the criterion referenced test have been tried out in pilot studies, reliability may be determined be it test-retest and/or split half reliability. If two forms of the criterion referenced test are available, a pilot study may be conducted to determine alternate forms reliability.

Outcomes based curricula emphasize students showing what has been learned from test results only. Observable, verifiable test results from each student are necessary. Schools, states, and the lay public desire to know in numerical terms what a student has learned. Objective reporting of each student's achievement becomes a necessity. Guesswork is eliminated. Teacher's proficiency is evaluated in terms of how well students do on the criterion referenced tests. The teacher is then held accountable for student achievement in terms of having attained an adequate number of behaviourally stated objectives.

Outcomes based education lists and states the following advantages for their advocated beliefs:

1. verifiable, objective results are available to demonstrate whether students are achieving at an adequate level;
2. teachers need to select learning activities aligning with the predetermined behaviourally stated objectives. The teacher needs pedagogy skills to choose activities so that students may attain objectives. Teachers are responsible for learner progress;
3. inputs such as teachers with high levels of college/ university education, money spent on students for schooling, among others, are not relevant. Only the ends of instruction are salient.

Disadvantages given for outcomes based education include the following:

1. parents, the lay public, and students themselves are not accountable for the latters achievement in school;
2. money spent on education is greatly slighted, since only student achievement is emphasized. Money spent on inputs such as teachers' salaries, teaching materials, and needed building repairs may be deemed unnecessary in a strict outcomes based system of instruction;
3. school curricula become stultified with predetermined objectives be they state mandated or district determined instructional management systems.

Pertaining to measurement of intended outcomes versus goal-free evaluation, McNeil[1] wrote:

> In the past Ralph Tyler told evaluators that it was impossible to decide whether a particular test would be appropriate for appraising a certain programme until the objectives of the programme had been defined and until the kinds of situations

that would give an opportunity for this behaviour to be expresses were identified. Tyler recommended checking each proposed evaluation device against the objectives and construction or devising methods for collecting evidence about the student's attainment of these objectives.

More recently, Micheal Scriven moved beyond Tyler's concern for data about intended outcomes to a concern for all relevant effects. His approach is called goal-free evaluation. This evaluation does not assess a situation merely in terms of goal preferences. It is evaluation of actual effects against a profile of demonstrated needs. It is offered as a protection against the narrow vision of those close to the programme, against harmful side effects, missed new priorities, and overlooked achievement. To the extent that Scriven's approach is used, more evaluative measures will have to be used. Selection of these measures will be difficult, for there are thousands of such devices. Practicality will probably dictate the use of measures that assess most intended outcomes and a limited number of possible side effects.

Tuition Voucher System

Without tuition voucher systems, parents may select the school for their son or daughter is attend, be it the local school or one further removed from home base. Parents need to be well informed about schools where quality education is provided. Otherwise, intelligent choices cannot be made pertaining to selecting a quality school for the offspring to attend. Information on schools and teachers with a high rating should be available. Heresay and opinion are not adequate.

Educational opportunities need to harmonise with the learning style of the student, be it visual, auditory, or kinesthetic approaches. Also, a student may be concrete, semi-concrete, or symbolic, (abstract oriented in learning). Schools may be classified in terms of emphasizing the basics, activity, centered curricula, or utilizing the community and society to provide the majority of learning opportunities for students.

The market place economy presents a model for the voucher system. The free enterprise system advocates consumer selecting, from among alternatives, what to buy. With the voucher system, parents select the kind of education desired for their son or daughter. Bad teachers then will be weeded out with no demand for their services. An analogy might be made here with consumers shopping in the market place. Bad products are not purchased and thus eliminated. Word gets around which products are bad and which are worthy of purchasing.

In traditional means of grouping for instruction, the principal of the school might well do the selecting of students for a given classroom and teacher. No input from parents is in evidence in making decisions pertaining to which classroom and teacher any particular student will have.

Advantages given for emphasizing the voucher system include the following:

1. decision making by parents is a definite possibility in choosing a perceived worthwhile curriculum for the son or daughter;
2. possibilities exist for harmonizing the students style of learning with that of the chosen school and teacher;
3. the profession of teaching is challenged for members to offer the best objectives, learning opportunities, and appraisal procedures for students.

Disadvantages given for opposing the voucher system include the following:

1. all teachers within diverse school systems should offer a curriculum of excellence, rather than those chosen by parents only;
2. the market economy of free enterprise cannot be compared to the educational arena. Quality education is not a commodity which can be measured numerically. There are diverse philosophies of education which might be implemented in teaching-learning situations. These include behaviourism with its predetermined measurably stated objectives for student attainment, humanism with its open-ended curriculum involving learner input, task analysis incorporating a planned sequence of objectives for student achievement, as well as a project method emphasizing an experience curriculum. Precise measuring of student achievement through testing is not advocated by selected

philosophies of education such as humanism and the project method;

3. parents may not identify the best curriculum possible for their offspring through the voucher system.

Pertaining to the voucher plan, Shepard and Ragan[2] wrote:

> In 1971 the Office of Economic Opportunity (OEO) granted funds for a feasibility study of the Voucher Plan to the public schools of Gary, Indiana; Seattle, Washington; and Alum Rock, California. This plan financed schools through a direct payment to parents of a voucher of a predetermined value. The parents would then select a school and present the voucher or payment for their child's schooling. These districts have discontinued the plans;
>
> Within this plan, a school district establishes an open enrolment policy and provides a choice to the parents in terms of the kind of school programmes offered. For example, one school unit might be traditional in organization, curriculum, control, and so on; another might be non-traditional and open; another might be patterned after Montessori. In 1974, Philadelphia had 110 alternative programme schools serving 7,500 children from ages 10-18.

Common Learnings for All Students

Selected educators emphasis that all students have access to the same subject matter. If this were not done, an elite group may be educated with the most sophisticated knowledge whereas others may have simpler subject matter to be in the offing for acquisition. Those with complex subject matter in the repertoire will then achieve at a higher level in education throughout the elementary through undergraduate school years. Students who acquired content on a lower achievement level will, no doubt, become more menial workers in the future at lower paying jobs.

Regardless of ability levels, each student would then have access, within the framework of teaching-learning situations, to the same/similar facts, concepts, and generalizations. No student would be ostricized from a curriculum of equity, equality, and excellence.

The concept of equality is emphasized in the Declaration of Independence—"For all men are created equal." With equality as a foundation concept in the Declaration of Independence, students need to experience a curriculum of equity. Equity stresses each student being of equal worth. A two tier society of the elite and the "hewers of wood and the drawers of water" should not exist.

Advocates of a common curriculum for all students believe that:

1. democratic tenets are inherent whereby all learners experience the same curriculum regardless of race, creed ability levels, and socio-economic levels;
2. all students have opportunities to secure the same subject matter so that discrimination in future jobs, occupations, and professions does not occur due to curricular school experiences;
3. respect for each student is evidence with equity in the curriculum. Equality of individuals receiving the same curriculum makes it so that students are not segregated in the school setting.

Disadvantages given for emphasizing a common curriculum for all students might be the following:

1. slow learners may not attach meaning and thus fail to understand what has been taught to the gifted and talented;
2. much optimism is expressed by educators who believe slow learners can achieve as much as the talented and gifted. The optimism may not be warranted;
3. individual differences among learners are violated in a common curriculum, especially if the same academic knowledge is taught to all students.

The Basics in the Curriculum

Numerous educators and the lay public emphasize a basics curriculum. With the basics, essential content is to be attained by students. The irrelevant and the frivolous are to be eliminated. What is deemed vital subject matter should be taught. Values clarification and moral education would be eliminated as well as literature emphasizing swear words, vulgarity, and sex.

The basics are defined differently by educators and the lay public. There is a lack of agreement as to what is meant by the basics. Some would define the basics as represented by reading, writing, and arithmetic. Reading and writing could be utilized as major methods in teaching science, history, and geography. However, academicians would not favour science, history, and geography as curriculum areas becoming reading classes.

The President of the United States, Senators, and Representatives have called for a return to the basics. They never defined what returning to the basics consists of. "Returning to the basics" has become a slogan and is to be substituted for what is deemed evil in education. For basics to be taught, agreements need to exist as to which objectives are to be emphasized therein. For example, in the teaching of reading, is phonics instruction a basic? If so, how much phonics should be taught? Thus several workbooks of solid phonics content could be completed for each of the kindergarten through grade three levels or years of instruction. In degrees, less emphasis could also be placed upon teaching phonics and the basics would still be in evidence.

Advantages in emphasizing the basics could

1. result in making thorough studies by educators and the lay public to determine which these basics truly are.
2. emphasize teaching what is vital, salient, and relevant.
3. eliminate what is perceived to be trivial and insignificant.

Disadvantages given for a basics curriculum might well be the following:

1. the scope of the curriculum should have adequate breadth to provide an education which assists students to develop well intellectually, emotionally, socially, and physically;
2. conservatism may be so in evidence that higher levels of cognition such as problem solving as well as critical and creative thinking are greatly minimized;

3. philosophical ideologies may stress the basics so that questioning of weaknesses in society are not in evidence. Keeping the status quo of the present system of government and economic system might be a motive for enforcement of sticking to the basics in the curriculum.

Pertaining to the basics or essentials, Bagley[3] wrote:

> A clear and primary duty of organized education at the present time is to recognize the fundamental character of the changes that are already taking place, and to search diligently for means of counteracting their dangers. Let us repeat that an educational theory meet to these needs must be strong, virile, and positive, not feeble, effeminate, and vague. The theories that have increasingly dominated American education during the past generation are at basis distinctly of the latter type. The Essentialists have recognized and still recognize the contributions of real value that these positive elements can be preserved in an educational theory which finds its basis in the necessary dependence of the immature upon the mature for guidance, instruction, and discipline. This dependence is inherent in human nature. "What has been ordained among the prehistoric protozoa," said Huxley, "cannot be altered by act of Parliament"- nor, we may add, by wishful thinking of educational theorists, however sincere their motives. "Authoritarianism" is an ugly word. But when those who detest it carry their laudable rebellion against certain of its implications so far as to reject the authority of plain facts, their arguments, while well adapted perhaps to the generation of heat, became lamentably lacking in light.

Holding Teachers Accountable

Considerable emphasis is placed upon holding teachers accountable for what students have achieved. With the accountability movement, precise measurably stated objectives have been determined on the state level or/and the district level (instructional management systems) for learner attainment. It is up to the teacher to select learning activities aligned with the predetermined objectives. Criterion referenced tests, developed on the state or district level, are used to measure student achievement to determine if objectives have been achieved. Percentile ranks are usually given to indicate at which level each student is achieving. Generally, higher scores are wanted from each student for sequential school years. The teacher is held accountable for students doing well on tests.

Teachers within the accountability movement do not choose the objectives nor the appraisal procedures to ascertain learner progress. They must select learning activities and must meet expectation results from student achievement.

Advantages given for accountability movements in education include the following:

1. teachers must take their responsibilities seriously to emphasize time on task for students;
2. teachers need to realize that test results from students reflect the quality of teaching and learning emphasized in the classroom;
3. teachers need to be concerned about what the lay public believes about public schools and student achievement.

Disadvantages for having accountability systems in education are the following:

1. It is not fair to hold each teacher accountable for students achieving the same/similar number of objectives. Not all students have similar abilities, achievement levels, interests, purposes, and capabilities;
2. Socio-economic levels of students can vary much from room to room, or building to building. Students cannot do well in school if poverty or near poverty levels exist in the home setting;
3. Will teaching for the test be an end result of the accountability movement? If teachers feel threatened by salary differentiation due to test results of students taught, and excess amount of pressure may be put on the instructor. If discipline problems abound in a classroom, students cannot achieve well. A roomful of slow learners also makes it unfair to compare one teacher against another who has more talented and motivated students.

Pertaining to excellence in education, Stevens and Wood[4] wrote:

> We speak often of excellence today, as an ideal for schools to emulate. The most discussed of the recent education reports link the term to standards, discipline codes, curricular requirements, and insurance against teacher judgements. Apparently, some people think we can "teacher-proof" classrooms. Few acknowledge that a school's chances for achieving excellence—its excellence potential—is very much a matter of its organization and procedures. These determine the kind of overall environment the school constitutes, which, in turn, determines whether excellence will set an apathetic tone, and the most extensive sharing may be relief at the sound of the last bell;
>
> Excellence cannot be mandated. It cannot be imposed on any institution, nor can its participants be coerced into pursuing it. Excellence emerges as a quality of the particular goals and norms chosen, the understandings and expectations created and shared by a group of people. It is the commitments of the participants which is the key. More precisely, institutional excellence is not so much a matter of individual values, as of norms participants share, norms which define the crucially important climate or ethos, the moral order, of a school. The excellence challenge then is a matter of generating an environment conducive to a shared commitment of excellence.

Education Bankruptcy Laws

Selected states presently such as Kentucky, New Jersey, and Massachusetts have educational bankruptcy laws. Thus if on the state level, a school district is declared bankrupt educationally, the following situations exist:

1. school district achievement of students has fallen below an acceptable level;

2. student test results, be it norm referenced or criteria referenced, has fallen below a minimum level.

It is difficult to say what an acceptable level of achievement is or should be when observing test results. Basing proper student achievement on test results limits the scope of the evaluation process. There are additional methods to utilize in appraising students, other than through testing. Through discussions, written products and oral reports, art and construction projects, additional approaches to appraise learner achievement are in evidence.

Testing to determine student achievement is quite popular in the United States. Selected educators and the lay public believes strongly in test results to determine student achievement. Also, teacher effectiveness may be measured by observing student's test results. Teacher accountability is involved when appraising learner test results.

Advantages provided for using test results to determine if a school is bankrupt educationally are the following:

1. objective results of student progress are then utilized. With test scores of students, data exists in terms of how well learners are achieving in a district. Test results may then be utilized to determine if a school or school district is educationally deficient and bankrupt;
2. subjectivity is then minimized to make judgements about deficiencies in school achievement;
3. the lay public accepts test results to determine how well teachers are doing in teaching students;

Disadvantages given for using test results to determine educational bankruptcies of schools are the following:

1. test results be it norm referenced or criterion referenced are not adequate to determine learner progress;
2. any approach to evaluate student progress may not be adequate to determine achievement. In addition to the school curriculum, other factors enter into the picture when assessing reasons for student achievement such as the home and local environments, ability levels of learners, socio-economic level facts, and personal motivation to achieve, grow, and learn;
3. local districts may not spend adequately to support the educational enterprise be it liveable salaries for teachers, audio-visual materials, and other teaching supplies, para-professionals to assist teachers in the classroom, appropriate buildings and facilities for instructional purposes, as well as parental support for schools.

Pertaining to testing, James William Noll[5] wrote:

Mental measurement and scientifically-grounded assessment instructions date back to the beginnings of the 20th century as part of a general movement to devise a "science of education." John Dewey, for one, was skeptical about the claims of measurement advocates, once comparing their efforts to pig-weighing on his grandfathers farm in Vermont. It seems that grandpa would place a pig at one end of a balancing board and then pile rocks on the other and until the two weights were perfectly equal. Then he would guess that weight of the rocks;

Somewhat similarly, the current dispute over measurement concerns whether at art of teaching and the art of learning can be fairly assessed by the science of testing. W. James Popham, an advocate of standardized testing, contends that high-quality testing problems are essential to the survival of public schooling. The tax-paying public has exerted great pressure for more concrete evidence of performance in light of what is seen as a decline in standards over recent decades;

Opponents raise the questions about the quality of fairness of current tests and about the effects of test re-test competition on both students and schools. Banesh Hoffman's 1962 book, The Tyranny of Testing, first posed these concerns. More recently, Andrew J. Strenio, Jr., in his 1981 book The Testing Trap, attacks meritocratic competitiveness, the perpetuation of the fear of failure, curricular manipulation by test makers, the distortion of the teaching process, and the "branding" of children which emanate from an overemphasis on standardized test results. Harold Berlak of the Public Education Information Network offers a case against the heavy current dependence on standardized examinations in an article entitled "Testing in a Democracy" (Educational Leadership, October 1985). He contends that such testing reduces learning to multiple choice items which trivialize knowledge, that many of the tests are written by experts who are remote from the classroom and often from the subject matter, and that teachers are spending more and more time teaching tests.

Financing School and Education

How should the public schools be supported financially? Where should the money come from to educate students in the school setting? In society, the slogan may be "Lets get government off our backs and out of our pockets." Or, "Read my lips, no new taxes" may be another slogan in society.

Holding taxes down seems to be normative, according to the New Right in society. The New Right believes strongly in supporting a perceived free enterprise system. Deregulation laws and rules are the order of the day do keep costs down and profits up for leaders in the free enterprise system. With lower takes, profits in a free enterprise state will be greater. With more profits for owners and managers in the business world, profit will trickle down to those lower on the wealth hierarchy, according to advocates of free enterprise. All will then benefit in society as the profits from big business provide an increased number of jobs and higher salaries for workers. Workers may then buy more goods and services, thus creating more jobs in society. With more profits for the wealthy and higher salaries for workers, an increased amount in dollars and cents goes into the federal treasury from taxable income.

The philosophy of big business is to cut red tape (laws, rules, and regulations) and keep income taxes low so that more profit and wealth goes to the owner or entrepreneur.

Businesses want quality education, but at the same time want reduced electrical, water, and rent costs, as well as other benefits, from a city where an economic establishment will be set up. Corporations may wish to spend more on defence within a nation so that the industrial-military complex will work in partnership. Profits then from governmental defence contracts go to big business and corporations.

The federal government has had grave problems even attempting to agree on means of balancing the budget. With a national debt of three trillion dollars and an annual budget deficit presently of one hundred eighty billion dollars, the federal government continues to cut away in spending money for education. State governments have a difficult time emphasizing a balanced budged, regardless of the calender year involved. The state sales tax is regressive indeed. Rich and poor pay the same per cent when goods and services are purchased and sales tax is to be added. A third source of revenue for the school is the local property tax. Amount of property which is taxable presents many weaknesses. For example, a farmer struggling to make a living with low livestock and grain prices may have much farm machinery and a limited amount of farming land. Yet a high investment in farm machinery is necessary to do farm work. The machines include tractors, combines, plows, harrows, and grain drills, among others.

Which kind of taxes then should be utilized to finance the costs of education?

1. The income tax based on ability to pay?
2. The state sales tax whereby each pays six per cent?
3. The property tax whereby the income from work involving the taxable property may be very low or exceedingly high.

What should be done if the lay public continually votes down more money for maintenance, new buildings, liveable teachers' salaries, and necessary teaching supplies?

1. Should district judges enforce laws or rules whereby residents within a district must tax themselves more heavily to pay for needed costs in education?
2. Should each state set or establish laws to pay for leaky roofs, replace steam radiator units that do not provide proper heat in winter, and to pay for safe playground equipment, among other needed items? Members of a sate department of educational could inspect complaints and provide written reports. Immediate action would need to be given to complaint items from the written report.
3. If regressive taxes such as the sales tax, property tax, gasoline tax, and exercise taxes are continually approved of by state and national legislators , should judges and courts mandate and progressively increases income tax?

Categories of Students to be Educated

How much money should be spent on educating the gifted, the average achiever, the slow learner, as well as the handicapped student? Financial support can be shifted from one category to the other, such as from funding the gifted to the handicapped.

In 1975, Congress passed and sent to the President for signature The Education for All Handicapped Children Act" bill and law. This law also known as PL 94-142. Major provisions of PL 94-142 include the following:

1. all students are entitled to an appropriate free education, regardless of handicaps possessed;
2. each student is to be placed in the least restricted environment. Thus, a handicapped student can be placed in a regular classroom for all part of each school day;
3. an IEP (Individual Educational Programme) needs to be written and approved for each mainstreamed pupil. The IEP consists of a set of clearly stated objectives for each mainstreamed child to achieve during the school year. The IEP is written at the beginning of the school year and should be approved by the classroom teacher, the parent (s), the school principal, and the special education teacher.

The classroom teacher then needs to provide for a wide range of pupil achievement with mainstreaming implemented. A heterogeneous set of pupils is then taught ranging from the gifted and talented to the mainstreamed educationally mentally retarded.

Since 1975 with the passing of the Education for all Handicapped Students, money for instruction as moved from teaching gifted/talented, average, and slow learners to programmes for the handicapped. Generally, the cost for educating a handicapped student is three to four times higher than for a regular student. Why? Increased services are provided to handicapped students, as compared to others. Thus problems with speech, hearing, dyslexia, learning, behavioural disorders, among other services provided to the handicapped, cost money.

The ratio of handicapped per teacher is low, usually five to eight students per teacher. An aid must assist the teacher of the handicapped. Special facilities such as a restroom per class of handicapped students is also needed. Special bus service is needed to transport the handicapped throughout the day.

There may be one handicapped student per teacher such as in the case of autism, or extreme emotional problems possessed by the student.

When the Education for All Handicapped Students law was passed, the federal government agreed to pay for forty per cent of the costs for education of the handicapped. The federal government instead has paid approximately fourteen per cent of the cost for implementing the Education for All Handicapped Students law.

With the tremendous shift of money spent in public school education from regular to handicapped students, numerous questions need to be answered.

1. How can all categories of students, regular and handicapped, be funded so each learner might achieve in an optimal manner?
2. Which objectives, learning opportunities, and appraisal procedures would guide each student to learn as much as capabilities and motivation permit?
3. Which materials of instruction are needed to assist each student to learn as much as possible?
4. What needs to be done to prepare each student to life well in society?
5. How can each student attain optimally in physical, emotional social, and intellectual development?
6. Which psychology of instruction, i.e. humanism or behaviourism, would assist learners to achieve objectives effectively in school?
7. Which philosophy of education should instructors utilize to stress adequate learner progress?
8. How should students be grouped for instruction, i.e. heterogeneously or homogeneously?

Pertaining to mainstreaming, Royer and Feldman[6] wrote:

> What were the disadvantages of traditional special education that led to such an upheaval? The need for change was made clear in an influential paper by Lloyd Dunn in 1968. In the paper, he

argued that there were four major reasons for abandoning the tradition of segregating handicapped children for purposes of schooling. First, any separate tracking system is likely to be inferior if it is meant to service some minority group. For instance, the best equipment and resources are likely to be diverted for majority group usage—in this case, non-handicapped populations. Second, Dunn suggested that there are no data to support the efficacy of special classes for handicapped students. Research that has examined such factors as academic achievement, self-concept, social adjustment, and personality has generally failed to discern any advantages for special needs children placed in special education, as opposed to regular, classes. Thus, it could be argued that the effort and cost of providing special classes is unwarranted;

A third argument against the use of totally segregated special education classes involved the issue of labeling students—as "mentally retarded," "handicapped," "special," etc. There is good evidence that labeling students can lead to the development of a set of negative expectations regarding their capabilities, which in turn can lead others to behave in ways that actually cause these expectations to be fulfilled. Moreover, being thus labeled can lead to a decrease in peer acceptance and self-concept. For instance, one study found that subject presented with an example of behaviour supposedly carried out by a student labeled "mentally retarded" rated the behaviour significantly less positively than when the behaviour was carried out by a student who was not so labeled and was thus assumed to be "normal" (Cook and Wollersheim, 1976).

Perhaps the most compelling argument suggested in Dunn's 1968 paper concerned the availability of new and improved teaching techniques. For example, individualized curriculum methods, in which the teacher provides special material geared to the level of each student, were becoming more common. Moreover, many teachers were adopting programmed learning based on operant learning principles. With instruction already becoming more individualized for all children, handicapped children could more easily be integrated into regular classrooms.

Teacher Education

Different schools of thought exist pertaining to the ideal plan for universities to follow in preparing teachers for the public schools. The traditional plan for the four year baccalaureate degree (BSE) has been something like the following for preparing secondary school teachers:

1. fifty semester hours of course work is general education;
2. thirty semester hours of course work in the major;
3. thirty semester hours of course work in professional education classes, preteaching experiences, and student teaching;
4. fifteen hours of electives in course work.

The four year BSE degree requirements area adhered to by most states in the union as being the minimal requirements which need to be met to be an elementary or secondary school teacher.

A traditional four year BSE in elementary education degree may be represented by the following requirements:

1. fifty semester hours of general education, required for all preparing to become teachers, be it elementary or secondary levels;
2. forty semester hours of course work in a single academic discipline leading to a minor;
3 forty semester hours in professional education classes, preteaching and field experience, as well as student teaching;
4. fifteen semester hours of elective classes.

Within any programme of teacher education, be it traditional or modern, the following standards are recommended:

1. more rigor and challenge in course work and practical experiences;
2. high expectations of students;
3. accreditation from leading teacher education consortiums;
4. quality control of the teacher education degree programme;

5. adequate evaluation of student progress and achievement;
6. revisions made as the need arises;
7. research results incorporated into the academic and professional education curriculum;
8. minimal entry levels into the degree programme, such as high Scholastic Aptitude Test (SAT) results and grade point average from high school. The high grade point average should be cumulative on the college/university levels;
9. competency tests to notice if a student possess prerequisite knowledge necessary for any teacher;
10. a committee which appraises student knowledge, skills, and attitudes needed to become a professional teacher.

The Holmes Group whose members come from leading research universities in the United States emphasize all prospective teachers secure a four year degree (Bachelor of Arts) in an academic subject area. The four year programme stresses an academic major as well as a minor together with elective courses. All course work represents the liberal arts and is non-vocational. The Holmes Group, named after Dr. Henry Holmes late Dean of the Harvard University School of Education, believes that a liberal arts degree must first be completed before teacher education is begun. Regardless of which level the prospective teacher will teach, each needs a liberal arts degree as a foundation, according to the Holmes Group. The fifth year, beyond the four year liberal arts degree, emphasizes students taking professional education classes, observation and gradual participation in classroom setting with students in the public schools, as well as participation in student teaching and internships.

Another model for preservice education emphasizes a five year programme terminating in a master's degree. The five year programme would integrate the liberal arts and education course work. Thus, a prospective teacher may experience working with pupils during the very first semester of college/university study, along with taking a few liberal arts classes. A goal here would be to evaluate if the university student truly wants to pursue a degree leading to becoming a fully licensed, certified teacher. Perhaps, the prospective teacher evaluates the self during these early experiences with children that he/she is not interested in teaching. Purpose or reasons for teaching may be lacking. During the early semesters of university training is an excellent time for students to pursue a different vocation, other than teaching, if evidence warrants this should be done. It is costly in time and money to pursue a programme of study which will be dropped. The student will then need to pursue a different degree programme, thus losing credit hours in the process.

With an integrated liberal arts/education programme of course work, the university student has increased opportunities to relate content, rather than perceiving isolated bits of information. An academician might also be able to demonstrate at selected intervals how specific academic subject matter should be taught to students. Dr. James Conant in the latter 1950's emphasized the clinical professor being able to show prospective teachers how academic content can be taught to pupils in the public schools.

Questions which need to be raised pertaining to a five year programme of teacher education include the following:

1. Will students have the needed finances to pursue a five year degree in teacher education?
2. Are salaries of beginning teachers with the five year programme completed, commensurate with money spent on education for a four year degree?
4. Can prospective teachers complete in four years that which is necessary to become a professional instructor?
5. Should the four year bachelor of arts (BA) be completed first of furnish subject matter knowledge for student teaching on the fifth year or master of arts (MA) level? Or, should relationship of the liberal arts and teacher education be correlated on either that BSE or MA degrees?
6. What makes for a quality teacher education programme, other than BSE or MA degree requirements?

7. How can quality in teacher education be developed and maintained, other than in listed courses for either a four or five year degree programme?
8. How can quality instructors of course work and supervisors of student teaching be in evidence?
9. Which materials of instruction, reading and audio-visual sources, assist in developing a teacher education programmes of excellence?
10. How can accrediting agencies monitor teacher evaluation programmes so that quality control is in evidence?

Student Teaching in Teacher Education

Diverse philosophies of student teaching are emphasized in university schools of education. Quality student teaching programmes should prepare the intern for being fully licensed, certified teacher. The intern should experience the entire gamut of activities which a regular teacher is involved in continuously. Experiences in student teaching should reflect that which is recommended from the philosophy of education and the psychology of education. Haphazard, unplanned experience in student teaching should not be in evidence.

Mentor teachers, to guide student teachers, should be selected carefully. Mentor teachers should be able to

1. work in a collegial manner with student teachers.
2. guide student teachers to develop quality objectives, learning activities, and appraisal procedures for pupils in the elementary and secondary classrooms.
3. supervise student teachers effectively in teaching-learning situations.
4. assist student teachers to provide for individual differences among pupils.
5. encourage student teachers to appraise their own progress in terms of desired criteria.
6. facilitate student teacher utilization of audio-visual materials.

7. stimulate student teachers to emphasize higher level of cognition such a critical and creative thinking as well as problem solving in teaching pupils.
8. have seminars for the prospective teacher to participate in with the sharing of ideas with other student teachers.
9. motivate student teachers to visit with the share ideas with diverse instructors in the school setting.
10. emphasize inquiry methods of instruction in the student teaching experience.

There are numerous unresolved issues in stressing quality in the student teaching experience:

1. How long should the prospective teacher gain new skills in the preservice student teaching programme? Universities may require one eight week period, one semester, or an entire school year;
2. How might quality mentor teachers be selected to assist student teachers to develop into being true professionals? A related issue pertains to who should choose mentors, be it the student teacher, the university supervisor of student teachers, the director of university student teachers, or principals in public schools;
3. Should a performance based programme of student teaching be in evidence or should a more open-ended philosophy prevail whereby objectives emerge within the student teaching programme?
4. If the services of the mentor prove to be ineffective in supervising student teachers, how should this situation be resolved?
5. Which standards should be utilized to determine if a student teacher has not mature adequately to become a fully licensed regular teacher?
6. If a student teacher does poorly in the classroom, what procedures are needed to correct the problem? Who should diagnose difficulties inherent to determine if the student teacher should continue in practice teaching?

7. What is the role of the director of student teaching in assisting the university supervisor to work with weak student teachers or ineffective mentor teachers?
8. How should the quality of services by the university supervisor of student teaching be evaluated?
9. Which procedures should be utilized to appraise performance of the mentor teacher?
10. How might a quality programme of inservice education for mentor teachers be implemented?

SUMMARY

Numerous issues in education were identified and discussed. These were:

1. an outcomes based education. The lay public might only want higher achievement (outcomes) from pupils with little emphasis placed upon inputs (adequate financial and material support) from the local public;
2. tuition voucher systems whereby parents choose the school and preferably the teachers for their children;
3. common learnings for pupils whereby a core of subject matter content needs to be mastered by all learners;
4. a basics curriculum, consisting of reading, writing, and arithmetic;
5. accountability of teachers, regardless of how accountable other segments in society are;
6. educational bankruptcy laws where a local district's pupils fall below agreed upon standards of achievement. The state superintendent may then take over the bankrupt district so that pupils may achieve at a higher level;
7. financing quality education in schools;
8. categories of students to be funded. Which category should be funded more adequately, i.e. the gifted, the average, or the handicapped?

9. teacher education requirements to become a fully licensed teacher;
10. philosophy of student teacher education.

REFERENCES

1. McNeil, John, D., *Curriculum: A Comprehensive Introduction*. Fourth Edition, Glenview, Illinois: Sott, Foresman/Little Brown Higher Education, 1990, pp. 247-248.
2. Shephard, Gene D. and Ragan, William B., *Modern Elementary Curriculum*. Sixth Edition. New York: Holt, Rinehart and Winston, 1982, p. 66.
3. Bagley, William C., *An Essentialist's Platform for the Advancement of American Education*. Educational Administration and Supervision, XXIV (April 1938), pp. 244-256.
4. Stevens, Edward and Wood George H., *Justice, Ideology, and Education: An Introduction to the Social Foundations of Education*. New York: Random House, 1987, p. 330.
5. Noll, James Wm., *Taking Sides: Clashing Views on Controversial Educational Issues*. Guilford. Connecticut: The Dushkin Publishing Group, Inc. 1987, pp. 294-295.
6. Royer, James M. and Feldman, Robert S., *Educational Psychology: Applications and Theory*. New York: Alfred A. Knopf, Inc., 1984, pp. 107-109.

7

Objectives in the Curriculum

Careful selection of objectives in the curriculum is a must. Objectives provide direction in terms of what students are to learn. Relevant objectives need to be chosen so that trivia is omitted. How can philosophy of education provide direction in objectives and goal selection?

Realism and the Selection of Objectives

Realist's base models of writing objectives on knowing the real world as it truly is. The learner is to receive a replica of the real world, as a result of instruction. Realism is based on empiricism in the world of science. Diverse academic disciplines such as astronomy, geology, chemistry, biology, zoology, botany, and physics, among others, present precise knowledge, not opinions nor values judgements. That which can be known precisely and empirically provides objectives of instruction in the curriculum. Mathematics, in its diverse branches, also contains exact content. Answers to problems in mathematics are either right or wrong, not on a continuum.

Since objectivity, empiricism, accuracy, and specificity exist as concepts in the scientific and mathematical world, one can know the real world in whole or in part as it truly is. Objectives of instruction, as and analogy, can be written with a high degree of specificity. Either a student has/has not achieved sequential ends as a result of instruction. Guesswork is not involved in teachers determining if objectives have/have not been achieved by students. The teacher may write the precise objectives, behaviourally stated, for students to attain in any curriculum area. Different states, by law, have had educators at the state level, write behaviourally stated objectives for student attainment. The objectives are then available to classroom teachers. Each teacher selects learning activities for students to achieve the objectives. Each activity aligns with the behaviourally stated objectives. Sequential activities for students need to be in offing. Criterion referenced tests (CRT's) measure against the objectives to determine if a student has/has not attained the precise end(s).

The following are examples of behaviourally stated objectives in selected curriculum areas:

1. The student will list in writing five causes for the Age of Discovery (social studies/social science);
2. The student will write a fifty word paragraph on how sedimentary rocks are formed (science);
3. The student will write a seventy-five word summary on *The five Hundred Hats of Bartholomew Cubbins (literature);*
4. The student will write five words/story problems and provide three different solutions to solve each problem (mathematics);
5. Given a variety of media, the student will develop a mural on content studied in an ongoing teaching unit (art);
6. The student will write a quatrain in poetry and set the words to music;
7. The student will demonstrate how to play a game from another nation. The game must involve psychomotor skills (physical education).

Each of the above named objectives contains an indicator or minimal level of achievement to determine if the student has or has not achieved and objective. For example, in the following behaviourally stated objective, the minimal level is underlined:

The appraisal procedures need to be valid in that they align with the stated objectives. Consistency in test results from students stresses the concept of reliability.

The following objective stresses a critical element in precision: The student will list in writing five causes for the Age of Discovery. Student achievement is measured in terms of having attained the minimal level in the indicator, as indicated by the underlined words.

Realists believe in:

1. precise statement of objectives;
2. alignment of learning activities for each stated objectives;
3. methods of instruction in emphasizing subject matter acquisition for student focus upon what is inside of the stated objective;
4. valid measurement techniques which align with each objective stressed in teaching and learning;
5. adequate structure in the curriculum to relate closely the objectives, learning activities, and measurement procedures.

Pertaining to Bertrand Russell's philosophy of realism, will Durant[1] wrote:

> What drew Russell to mathematics is, again, its rigid impersonality and objectivity; here, and here alone, is eternal truth, and absolute knowledge; the *A priori* theorems are the "Ideas" of Plato, the "eternal order" of Spinoza, the substance of the world. The aim of philosophy should be to equal the perfection of mathematics by confining itself to statements similarly exact, and similarly true before all experience. "Philosophical propositions. . . must be *a priori*." says this strange positivist. Such propositions will refer not to things but to relations, and to universal relations. They will be independent of specific "facts" and events; if every particular in the world were changed, these proportions would still be true. e.g., "if all A's are B's, and X is A, then X is a B": this is true whatever A may be; it reduces to universal and *a priori* from the old syllogism about the morality of Socrates; and it would be true if no Socrates, even if nobody at all, had ever existed. Plato and Spinoza were right:

"the world of universals may also be described as the world of the being. The world of being is unchangeable, rigid, exact, delightful to the mathematician, the logician, the builder of metaphysical systems, and all who love perfection more than life." To reduce all philosophy to such mathematical form, to take all specific content out of it, to compress it (voluminously) into mathematics—this was the ambition of the new Pythagoras.

Idealism and the Selection of Objectives

Idealists believe strongly in a liberal arts, subject centered curriculum. Vocational education in terms of jobs, professions, and occupations is emphasized beyond the under-graduate university curriculum and is definitely not a part of the liberal arts. Students on the elementary, junior high school, and secondary level so instruction need to achieve objectives reflecting social studies/social sciences, science, literature, mathematics, art, music and physical education as reflected in liberal arts and general education. Students need to achieve vital concepts and generalizations which reflect worthwhile ideas, according to idealism as a philosophy of education.

Intellectual development of the student comes first in curriculum development. Mental achievement must be inherent in student attainment of cognitive objectives. From the finite to the infinite represent goals for students to achieve on a continuum. An academically talented teacher assists students to achieve well intellectually and academically in the liberal arts. The liberal arts represent common learnings for all students, regardless of future careers to be followed. The liberal arts curriculum prepares students for the adult world. Thus an idea centered curriculum is basic for the future role of an adult in society. The teacher, as an idealist, needs to lock beyond the physical realm to determine that which is worth for students to learn. The mental exists beyond the material realm in the universe. Intelligence, will, and purpose exist beyond what can be experience by the senses. A Universal Mind exist beyond the here and now, as well as beyond the natural environment.

Mind is real and active in the pursuit of eternal truths. Thought and contemplation are needed to understand what is true, everlasting, and universal. The thinking mind reaches out to grasp eternal truths. Coherence (unity) of ideas is vital when testing ideas for truth and being true. With coherence, new ideas must be related to a larger whole to be true. Contemplation is important to achieve goodness, beauty, and truth.

The ultimate goal for everything is Perfection. The finite (limited) person through a study of the liberal arts moves increasingly in the direction of the Absolute (God or Universal Mind).

Students possess free will to pursue diverse choices. Wrong as well as right choices are made in life due to freedom of the will. Idealists do not emphasize precise, measurably stated objectives, as do realists. Idealism emphasizes general objectives for student achievement. Achieving of universals and generalizations harmonizes more so with general objectives as compared to measurably stated ends.

The idealist teacher, among others, has the following goals for student attainment:

To develop within the student:

1. an appreciation for vital subject matter knowledge;
2. a desire for life long learning in all academic subject matter areas;
3. a value system of wanting to achieve at an increasingly higher level;
4. a will and desire to learn, achieve, grow, and develop in the direction of the Infinite;
5. a feeling of wanting to develop toward an ideal. Character development is vital to the idealist. The ideal person increasingly becomes more like God or the Infinite.

Immanuel Kant[2] (1724-1804) in his essay *Right Acts Must Be Universalizable* wrote:

> ...Unless we wish to deny to the concept of morality all truth and all relation to a possible object, we cannot dispute that its law is of such widespread significance as to hold, not merely for men, but for all rational beings as such—not merely subject to contingent conditions and expectations, but with absolute necessity. It is therefore clear that no experience can give us

occasion to infer even the possibility of such apodeicitc laws. For by what right can we make what is perhaps valid only under the contingent conditions of humanity into an object of unlimited reverences a universal precept for every rational nature? And how could laws for determining our will be taken as laws for determining the will of a rational being as such—and only because of this for determining ours—if these laws were merely empirical and did not have their source completely *a priori* in pure, but practical, reason?

What is more, we cannot do morality a worse service than by seeking to derive it from examples. Every example of it presented to me must first itself by judged by moral principles in order to decide if it is fit to serve as an original example—that is, as a model; it can in no way supply the prime source for the concept of morality. Even the Holy One of the Gospel must first be compared with our ideal of moral perfection before we can recognize him to be such. He also says of himself: 'Why callest thou me (whom thou seest) good? There is none good (the archetype of the good) but one, that is, God (whom thou seest not).' But where do we get the concept of God as the highest good? Solely from the Idea of moral perfection, which reason traces *a priori* and conjoins inseparably with the concept of a free will. Imitation has no place in morality, and examples serve us only for encouragement... .

Experimentalism and the Selection of Objectives

Experimentalists believe that experience is all one can know about the real world. One cannot know the real world as it truly is, as the realists emphasize. Nor, can one know ideas only, about the real world as idealists believe. The world of experience is that which truly is all one can know of the natural/social world, according to experimentalists.

The curriculum of the experimentalist relates directly to life-like experiences. One experiences change in the real world. Change, rather than stability, is a key concept in experimentalism. Society is not the same yesterday, today, and forever. The natural/social environment changes and does not stay the same. With new inventions, ideas, customs, values, and beliefs, problems arise. No longer is the world the same eternally, by any means. With change surrounding the person, problems arise. New problems then need identification. With new problems identified, novel solutions are necessary. The old with its tried and true solutions no longer may work to solve one or more unique problems. Thus information needs acquisition from diverse kinds of reference sources in the data gathering process. Information must relate directly to the problem(s) identified.

After adequate data has been acquired, be it within a very short interval of time of a longer segment, the problem solver needs to develop a hypothesis. The hypothesis, and answer to the chosen problem, is tentative and subject to testing in a life-like situation. After testing, modification occurs, if needed.

Experimentalists are very much aware of the tentativeness of each hypothesis and knowledge in general. What represent truth presently may well not represent truth tomorrow. New problems and experiences make for these changes.

Truth to an experimentalist stresses that which works in everyday experiences. Truth is not based on the *a priori*. *A priori* emphasizes that which has always been true and is not based on human experiences. *A priori* statements, according to the idealist, could be represented by answers to basic addition, subtraction, multiplication, and division facts. These have always been true regardless of experience by individuals in society according to idealism.

To an experimentalist, absolutes and the *a priori* do not exist. Rather, individuals interact with society and as this interaction occurs, new experiences are encountered. Each individual experiences. Collectively in groups, accounts of experiences are modified, changed, and refuted. The experiences generally represent dilemmas that transpired. Each dilemma provides a unique situation where exact paths of action are not known. One can lean upon past experiences to provide guidance and direction in terms of action and deeds to perform. Dilemmas generally represent new problematic situations requiring solutions.

Objectives to achieve in an experimentalist philosophy of teaching might well be the following:

1. critical and creative thinking to solve problems;
2. the societal arena being salient in problem identification;

3. actual testing of hypotheses to problems in life-like settings;
4. committee work to identify and solve problems;
5. elimination of dualisms such as interest and effort. Rather, interest provides for effort and becomes an integrated entity.

John Dewey wrote:

> It is the very nature of life to strive to continue in being. Since this continuance can be secured only by constant renewals, life is a self-renewing process. What nutrition and reproduction are to a physiological life, education is to social life. This education consists primarily in transmission through communication. Communication is a process of sharing experience till it becomes a common possession. It modifies the disposition of both parties who partake in it. That the ulterior significance of every mode of human association lies in the contribution which it makes to the improvement of the quality of experience is a fact most easily recognized in dealing with the immature. That is to say, while every social arrangement is educative in effect, the educative effect first becomes an important part of the purpose of the association of the older with the younger. As societies become more complex in structure and resources, the need of formal teaching and training grow in extent, there is the danger of creating an undesirable split between the experience gained in more direct associations and what is acquired in school. This danger was never greater than at the present time, on account of the rapid growth in the last few centuries of knowledge and technical modes of skill.

Whatever subject matter is needed, regardless of academic discipline involved, is utilized to solve problems. Separate academic disciplines for students to study is not important to an experimentalist. Unity of content is necessary to provide data for problem solving according to experimentalists.

Existentialism and the Selection of Objectives

Existentialism stresses a highly open ended curriculum. It is quite opposite of the measurably stated objectives and testing movement as advocated by realists.

Existentialism places major emphasis upon the student himself/herself when selecting objectives for teaching-learning situations. The learner is the focal point in curriculum development. The needs and interests of the student are paramount factors to consider in the curriculum. Societal needs are quite subordinate to the personal needs and interests of the student. Objectives of instruction then need to guide students to attain that which their personal needs and interests dictate.

Each student wishes to attain what is desired by the self. Optimal self-achievement might then be possible, if the inherent objectives reflect these ends. The teacher must provide a learning environment which assists students to attain humane goals of instruction. To attain humaneness and self-development, the school curriculum needs to stress subgoals for learner achievement. Thus each student needs to have adequate nutrition, proper clothing, and appropriate shelter. A safe environment for study, growth, and development is a must. Feelings of fear, alarm, anxiety and hurt are the antithesis of a safe environment. Furthermore, each student wants to be known for possessing some speciality, skill, or act which is deemed salient by others. To possess knowledge, skills, and attitudes desired by others, provides esteem for the involved student. Also, all students want to possess feelings of being accepted by others. Feelings of belonging and group adhesion are needed by all students.

The student then is a complex whole. There are many personal needs which must be fulfilled so that the student can learn, achieve, attain, and progress.

Existentialists advocate heavy student input into the curriculum. Students need to select, from among alternatives, which objectives to achieve and which to omit. The actual development of objectives for learners to attain should stress input from involved students. Each student needs to become proficient in decision-making. Life consists of making choices. Thus, the learner needs to be involved in determining objectives, as well as sequential ends to attain.

Objectives for student achievement within the framework of existentialism might well be the following:

1. to become skillful in the art of choosing and deciding;
2. to assume responsibility for choices made;
3. to accept others as having extremely high worth;
4. to realize self-fulfillment in terms of goals, learning opportunities, and appraisal procedures stressed in the curriculum;
5. to realize the concept of subjectivity being inherent in deeds, acts and thought emphasized in the school curriculum as well as in the societal arena.

Ralph Harper[4] wrote:

> Existentialism is, as the word implies, a philosophy of human existence. It arose early in the nineteenth century in response to a cultural climate in which Soren Kierkegaard observed that men had forgotten what it means to exist. Men had learned what it means to be one in a crowd, to be a mass-man; they had forgotten what it means to be an individual, that is, what it means to die, to suffer, to decide, to love. They had forgotten what it means to stand apart, as each man is born to stand apart, from the rest of the universe and from one's fellows. They had forgotten what it means to stand apart in need of a Judge and Redeemer.

Perennialism and the Selection of Objectives

Perennialists believe in looking to the past for objectives of instruction. That which has endured in time and place in the academic world is worthy of study. The recent and the modern may not become vital in time and place. It will take years and in diverse geographical regions to notice if the new endures in terms of academic standards.

The great minds and thinkers of the past have ideas worthy to study in any age. Ancient, medieval, the renaissance, and the age of enlightenment have given the modern world that which is vital yesterday, today, and forever. Objectives of instruction need to reflect the world of stability, the changeless, and the eternal. The transitory and the temporary need to be eliminated from the curriculum. A non-vocational curriculum also needs to be in evidence. The vocations should be emphasized after students have become well grounded in the classics, possibly on the graduate university level of instruction.

Great Minds of the past then have much to offer students in the curriculum. For students, the original in terms of the classics needs to be read, studied, and pondered over. Effort needs to be put forth in the studying the great ideas (great books) of the western world. A competent teacher of the classics needs to be in charge of stimulating students to participate in discussions, lectures, and seminars. The dedicated teacher is a master of classical literature and encourages students to develop well academically.

Since cultivation of the intellect is the primary objective of instruction, students needs to become proficient in delving into the abstract. Rational thinking and logic are involved. The concrete and the semi-concrete should be utilized as learning opportunities only if students achieve increasingly in the symbolic domain. Students should have ample opportunity to meditate and contemplate on that which is good, true, and beautiful. Higher cognitive objectives need to be emphasized within the framework of teaching-learning situations.

Objectivity can be achieved by students through rational thinking. Content studied may well be quite abstract; however universal ideas and generalizations come about through the utilization of the rational powers. By studying great ideas from outstanding thinkers of the past, the student experiences a liberal arts curriculum which is non-vocational. The liberal arts curriculum of studies may then emphasize student being rational or thinking individuals in a free society.

For objectives of instruction, the perennialist recommends:

1. a stimulating academic curriculum emphasizing vital, enduring ideas;
2. cultivation of rational powers to be the major goal of teaching;
3. a highly dedicated, academic teacher teaching students;
4. a core of subject matter content for student attainment, not an elective system;
5. adequate time be given for students to reflect upon acquired subject matter.

Pertaining to Mortimer Alder's *Paideia Proposal* (1982), Tanner and Tanner[5] wrote:

> The perennialist refusal to consider the nature of the learner in developing the curriculum is reflected in The Paideia Proposal. Instead of seeing childhood and youth as distinct phases of human development requiring uniquely appropriate learning experiences for effective growth, childhood and youth are regarded as obstacles to be gotten over as quickly as possible. "Youth itself is the most serious impediment—in fact, youth is an insuperable obstacle to being an educated person," declares the Proposal. The Proposal goes on the call for twelve years of basic schooling for all, capped by the Socratic study of great literary works and other works of art. This kind of learning "aims at raising the mind up from a lesser or weaker understanding to a stronger and fuller one," declares Alder, and the "art of the teacher depends on the teacher's understanding of how the mind learns by the exercise of its own power," declares Alder, as though the mind exists as a separate entity.

Marxism and the Selection of Objectives

Marxism believes in an ultimate classless society. This will occur when workers (proletariat) revolt against and overthrow the owners (bourgeoisie) of factories. With division of labour in factories, each worker to be proficient performs a single task over and over again. This makes for two classes in society, the worker and the wealthy entrepreneur. The worker receives less and less in wages due to labour saving equipment in factories. Subsistence wages are then paid to workers. With labour saving equipment brought in more and more into factories, many workers become unemployed. Workers are exploited and taken advantage of. Profit from production of workers goes to owners of factories. To keep exploited workers under control, strict laws are passed favouring the entrepreneur. Religious institutions also favour the wealthy entrepreneur. Churches may well favour a pure free enterprise system of economics. Thus the oppressed worker should be satisfied with his lot in life and wait for his reward in the hereafter (heaven). Marx believed that the personality of workers is shaped by the law of supply and demand as well from religious beliefs.

Marx believed in freedom of the individual. Freedom could only occur in a classless society where workers are the rulers.

Otherwise, the bourgeoisie would dominate the life of the proletariat with low wages and unacceptable standard of living.

Marxism might well emphasize the following objectives in the school curriculum:

1. the collective being more salient than individual endeavours. Goals of the group need implementation. What is emphasized in deeds and acts stresses the collective:
2. workers being more important than the entrepreneurs. In fact, entrepreneurs become parasites in collecting profits accruing from efforts of workers;
3. the lot of the poor resulting from exploitation for workers by entrepreneurs;
4. the wealthy living luxurios lifestyles whereas the poor live on or below subsistence levels;
5. laws and religious beliefs being designed to keep workers in their places.

Gross[6] wrote the following pertaining to the Hutterites in the United States and Canada, a communal society:

> The life of a member of a Hutterite community cannot be compared with the life of an ordinary citizen of the country who carries the whole responsibility of his affairs himself. Since the community is an assembly of many, the burdens are also put on the shoulders of many, as both abilities and needs are shared. On a one-for-all and all-for-one basis there is never a lack of organic unity and responsibility. The similarity of spirit and mind creates a united force for purposeful activity. The commune is a single organism, consisting of the one body and having one spirit and one heart.
>
> Whenever the Hutterites planned a migration to another country, it was simply for the reason of toleration and the question of military service. Their first question of the immigration authorised was regarding exemption from war service. They requested that as Christians and conscientious objectors, they be tolerated and totally exempt from the militia. If their request was refused, they would not consider the deal any further. On the other hand, if it was granted then further negotiations would take place, and they

praised God when it was possible to reach a satisfactory concordat, for they credited Him for it, as His hand was upon it.

SUMMARY

Each philosophy has definite goals to emphasize in the curriculum. Realism stresses its precise, measurably stated objectives of instruction. Idealists stress in idea centered curriculum in which mental and character development of learners become important. Experimentalism emphasizes problem identification and related solutions stressing the real world in society. Existentialists advocate a student centered curriculum with learners supported by teacher guidance choosing the means and ends of the instruction. Perennialists believe in a classical curriculum for students. Marxists emphasize a collective society in which workers become the decision-makers in society.

Diverse philosophical beliefs need to be understood and analyzed to realize their own implication for curriculum development. Each teacher and principal needs to be cognizant of philosophies utilized in the educational arena.

REFERENCES

1. Durant, Will, *The Story of Philosophy*. New York: Pocket Books, Inc. 1958. pp. 479-480.
2. Kant, Immanuel. *The Fundamental Principles of the Metaphysics of Morals*. New York: Hutchinson Publishing Group Ltd. (Translated by H. J. Paton), 1948.
3. Dewey, John. *Democracy and Education*. New York: The Macmillan Company. 1961. p. 9.
4. Harper, Ralph. *Significance of Existence and Recognition for Education in Modern Philosophies of Education*. Chicago: the University of Chicago Press. 1955. p. 215.
5. Tanner, Daniel., and Tanner, Laurel. *History of the School Curriculum*. New York: Macmillan Publishing Company. 1990. p. 333.
6. Gross, Paul S. *The Hutterite Way*. Saskatoon, Canada: Freeman Publishing Company Limited. 1965. pp. 171 and 123.

8

Designing the Curriculum

To design a quality curriculum can be a highly worthwhile endeavour. A curriculum needs to possess structure. The structure may consist of the basics or essentials or it can be quite open-ended. There are numerous ingredients then that need to go into curriculum development.

Separate Subjects versus Relationship of Academic Disciplines

A separate subjects curriculum emphasizes the teaching of specific units of study on history only, or any other singular social science discipline. Or in the sciences, the teacher could teach units on biology only, physics only, or any other academic division of subject matter content. Specific units could also be taught on particular academic disciplines within literature, language, and grammer, among others.

Teaching a unit of study to students emphasizing a particular academic solely, has its definite advantages. A teacher might then stress students acquiring facts, concepts, and generalizations in depth. To emphasize depth instruction requires time for these teaching-learning situations. A variety of learning activities are needed to guide learners to acquire each facet of worthwhile subject matter within an academic discipline. Depth teaching is always to be preferred as compared to survey procedures. With survey teaching many facts, concepts, and generalizations are taught within a selected interval of time. With depth teaching, fewer facts, concepts and generalizations are taught within that same interval of time. For each fact, each concept, and each generalization, variety in sequential learning opportunities are necessary. Pertaining to depth teaching in Theodore Sizer's Coalition of Essential Schools. Watkins[1] wrote:

> In what Mr. Sizer calls his "fantasy school," teachers would teach fewer subjects than they do now and teach them in greater depth. Students would be active learners—"student as worker," as Mr. Sizer puts it—and teachers would be coaches, not lecturers who deliver information;
>
> In addition, teachers would be responsible for no more than 80 students, rather than 175 or so, a number that Mr. Sizer says is common now. Only after students demonstrated mastery of the knowledge and skills of the school's curriculum would diplomas be awarded;
>
> "Good schools accept the convenience that no two kids are alike," says Mr. Sizer, elabourating on his ideal. "Seven kids may get the answer to a problem wrong, but it may be for seven different reasons;"
>
> To understand those reasons, "you have to know each student well enough to know why in each case," he says. "Kids learn in different ways. They are interested in different things. So you can't teach in one way;
>
> Mr. Sizer maintains that reducing the total number of subjects that students take in school is critical.
>
> "To get kids in the habit of using minds means giving them important questings and lots of time to struggle with them," he says. "One issue can't be knocked off in one day—tomorrow you will read the Bill of Rights and Friday there will be a test;"
>
> In a coalition school, he says, "you cover a lot less, but you do it thoroughly;
>
> "Less is more;"
>
> "This is all common sense," he adds. "It is nothing bizarre. What is bizarre is the way we run schools now;"
>
> The coalition's founder acknowledge that he was marked as an educational reformer in childhood;

"I grew up with parents who preached the word that you should leave the planet a better place than you found it," he says.

There are advantages in having and implementing a separate subjects curriculum. These include:

1. students becoming thoroughly familiar and highly knowledgeable about each single academic discipline;
2. deeper understanding of the discipline providing content for instruction;
3. sequence coming from one academic discipline without interference from other disciplines in a more correlated, fused, or integrated approach;
4. breadth of subject matter incorporating a single academic discipline making it possible for students to understand scope of content more adequately;
5. opportunities for students utilizing methods and procedures of acquiring information as emphasized by academicians in their academic areas of speciality.

If a teacher teaches a specific academic discipline only, such as in departmentalization plans of grouping students, he/she will tend to have had a strong academic background on the college/university level of under-graduate and graduate course work in content presently being taught.

Within each academic discipline, a logical sequence follows. For example, in a historical unit of study being taught, chronology in time is important for students to understand. A definite order in events occurred. The order or sequence needs emphasis. To improve understanding of an interval of time might well mean to have students attach meaning to subject matter being taught.

Somewhat toward the other end of the continuum, academic disciplines may be related in teaching-learning situations. A correlated curriculum tends to relate two academic areas. For example, when history is taught such as early explorers in the age of exploration, the regions (geography) explored could also be pinpointed on a map or globe. Fewer separate academic disciplines then need to be taught. Educational psychologists have long advocated that students perceive knowledge as being related. Increased retention of subject matter is then a possibility.

Further relationship of subject matter may be emphasized with the fused curriculum. Here, as an example, diverse social science disciplines such as history, geography, political science, economics, anthropology, and sociology may well be brought into a single unit of study. Thus in any nation being studied, the teacher can assist students to study:

(a) its history;

(b) the geographical setting;

(c) kinds and types of government (political science) in evidence;

(d) goods and services (economics) produced;

(e) the cultural arena (anthropology and sociology).

To stress the fused curriculum, students need to perceive the relationship of all these social science disciplines. With a fused curriculum, the teacher needs to relate diverse academic disciplines into a unity or oneness. Each discipline being taught separately is definitely not stressed. Rather, students are assisted to relate, not isolate, subject matter components. Pertaining to the fused (also called the broad-fields curriculum, Shepherd and Ragan[2] wrote:

> The curriculum areas of language arts and social studies were developed within this organizational pattern, and they characterize this type. The broad-fields or fusion pattern accepted the subjects of the correlated pattern, but adjusted the scope and sequence to achieve a greater integration of learning experiences. The classroom schedule had longer periods of time; transfer of learning was encouraged and rewarded within these longer blocks of study; and the method called "unit teaching" was developed. The units were subject-centered, but were planned to related skills, knowledges, and appreciations within these larger areas of study. This pattern also added emphasis to the

importance of pupil involvement, interest, and motivation as a positive factor in pupil achievement and curriculum planning;

An excellent example of the broad-fields type of organizations is found in the unified language arts programme. Instead of scheduling reading, writing, spelling, listening, and other separate subjects for approximately ten minutes each, a longer time (perhaps fifty minutes) is scheduled for language arts. Another example is found in the social studies. Instead of scheduling history, geography, economics and other separate subjects for a brief period each, a longer period is set aside for a united social studies programme.

Critics of the board-fields or fusion pattern for organizing the curriculum suggested that it was still to subject-centered and therefore did not provide for a fully integrated and interrelated learning experience. According to its critics, if this much adjustment in scope and sequence is good, why maintain a subject centered organization at all?

The integrated curriculum goes one step further than the fused curriculum. For example, science, mathematics, the humanities, art, and music are brought into the social studies curriculum as it is good to do so and guides students to achieve more optimally. The integrated curriculum is not emphasized for the sake of content integration, but rather as it increase student opportunities to secure increased meaning from subject matter that is perceived as being related.

Scope in the Curriculum

What should be taught in any instructional unit of study? The objectives of instruction should indicate breadth of content taught for a single lesson or an entire unit. The teacher could focus on knowledge objectives of instruction. The sum total of all the knowledge objectives emphasized would stress *scope* in the curriculum. A narrower or broader scope can be emphasized. Thus in science instruction, major emphasize could be placed upon zoology as a single curriculum area. The *scope* could be broadened to include botany. Additional academic disciplines could also be stressed. The scope then increasingly becomes broader. State mandated objectives, district-wide instructional management systems, approved curriculum guides and resource units might also determine the scope of a science course. Or it could be teacher judgement solely, that determines breadth of content in science instruction.

Time factors might also be involved in determining scope in the curriculum. If ample time is available to teach a specific curriculum area, the scope may well be broadened. Conversely, limited available time for teaching a subject matter area might well narrow the scope of the curriculum.

If student input is involved in curriculum development, much emphasis may then be placed upon student interests. Through learner questions raised in class or the use of teacher-pupil planning of learning opportunities, the student is assisting to determine the scope of the curriculum.

More specifically, the following procedures would answer the question of what is to be taught or the scope of the curriculum:

1. problems identified in an ongoing unit by students. Each problem area needs a committee to develop solutions. The total number of problems equals the scope of the curriculum emphasizing a problem solving philosophy;
2. tasks at diverse learning centers. At each center, four to five tasks may be typed on a card. An adequate number of centers with their respective stations is in evidence so that any student may select sequential tasks to pursue. Those not deemed purposeful, a student can omit;
3. subject matter in textbooks and workbooks selected by the classroom teacher could answer the question of *what* will be taught. The scope of the curriculum is reflected within the facts, concepts, and generalizations contained in the adopted textbook(s);
4. sequential lesson plans developed by the teacher. Here, the classroom teacher creatively develops each lesson

plan. Learning activities within each plan may be based upon the adopted textbook series and related workbooks. Or, no textbooks/workbooks are utilized. In either situation, other learning activities, than textbooks and workbooks, would predominate;

5. the basics, in any academic area taught, being identified by teachers, administrators, and curriculum directors.

Pertaining to student input into the curriculum when determining scope, Ediger[3] wrote about the following approaches:

1. discussing with pupils which units of study they wish to pursue;
2. having pupils assist in determing which problem areas to pursue within a unit of study introduced by the teacher;
3. listening to comments made by pupils as to what captures their interests; objectives, learning experiences, and evaluation procedures may be selected and evaluated based on student comments;
4. learning centers may be developed cooperatively by pupils with teacher leadership. The learning activities contained at each center would they largely determine what pupils are to learn.

Sequence in the Curriculum

When should selected facts, concepts, and generalization be taught in any unit of study? Answering the question of *when* stresses sequence. Any specific unit in science, should it be taught on the primary, intermediate, junior or senior high school levels? Within, for example the primary level should the science unit be taught on the kindergarten, first second, or third grade level? Further questions pertaining to sequence would state if the science unit should be taught first, second, third, fourth, and so on, within a particular grade level. Within the science unit, should listed objective one be stressed first, second, third, or higher ordinal levels within the hierarchy? To achieve listed objective number one, which learning activity should come number one, two, three, four, and so on? The reader will notice there are many problems involved in determining sequence to the curriculum.

Quality sequence is important in teaching since learners taught need to achieve optimally as continually as possible. When the objectives and learning opportunities move forward gradually in complexity, students have a better chance to achieve and learn. When subject matter to be acquired becomes too complex in sequence, failure as an end result tends to occur. If subject matter is too easy to attain, boredom on the part of students might well occur. It almost appears as if an optimal time is present for each student to acquire the new knowledge or skills, and yet be successful in ongoing endeavours to do so. Sequence in the curriculum then becomes a vital term in teaching-learning situations. Pertaining to sequence, Phenix[4] wrote:

> Since learning takes place over time, the materials of instruction have to be arranged in temporal sequence. Not everything can be studied at once; hence, decisions must be made about the order of instruction. How are these decisions to be made? What principles of sequence are available?
>
> It should be granted at once that to a degree the order of studies is arbitrary. There is no law of sequence that, if it were known, would prescribe exactly the succession of learning events. Education is in this respect like many of the affairs of ordinary life, in which the order of activities may be a matter of indifference. If one plans both to read a magazine and to run an errand, there may be no reason at all for doing one rather than the other first. Similarly, if it is decided that the curriculum is to include both music and painting, it may be a matter of indifference which comes first, it follows that, to some degree, accidental factors relating to historical traditions, personal inclinations, and available resources may properly be used to determine the sequence of studies and that many different, equally satisfactory orders can be devised.

> Granted this limited arbitrariness, it is still necessary to study the principles of sequence that govern a desirable curriculum. There are two kinds of sequence factors to be considered. One kind has to do with the psychological factors in learning, by which the order of studies is related to the order of human growth and development... . The other kind of sequence factors relate to the logic of what is to be learned... .

A logical sequence might be emphasized in teaching-learning situations. With a logical sequence, the teacher orders objectives for student attainment. From the simple to the increasingly more complex stresses a quality guideline to utilize in sequencing objectives in the curriculum. When arranging objectives in a logical sequence, the teacher determines, through examination and reason, which objective learners should attain first, followed in sequence by others. Teacher judgement is involved in making these decisions. Students basically have on input in making these decisions. Logic exists in the mind of the teacher, not students, in ascertaining the order of objectives for learner achievement.

Toward the other end of the curriculum, a psychological curriculum may be emphasized. With a psychological arranged order of objectives, the students is rather heavily involved in sequencing. Sequence resides within the student, not the teacher. The teacher is a guide and stimulator to encourage students to be active participants in determining the order of objectives. A humane learning environment for students is involved when these learners have a voice in selecting and ordering objectives. Students may then make choices and decisions. A student centered curriculum is involved when a psychological sequence is in evidence.

With a learning center philosophy of instruction, the student may select sequential tasks to complete. An adequate number of tasks at diverse centers are available so that the learner may omit those not possessing perceived purpose. The student is the chooser of task to complete, not the teacher. To plan the centers, the teacher may determine tasks with student input. A psychological curriculum is in evidence with students selecting sequential tasks.

Separate from a learning center philosophy, student-teacher planning of objectives, learning activities, and appraisal procedures may be emphasized. Through cooperative planning, the student orders his/her own experiences be it in the form of objectives, activities, or appraisal method. Psychologically, the student sequences what will be learned within planning sessions.

Individualized reading may also stress a psychological curriculum. On any grade level and within any unit of study, the student selects sequential library books to read. A wide variety of books on different topics and reading levels needs to be in the offing. Learners need to have opportunities to select library books which are of personal interest and possess meaning. The teacher intervenes to choose a library book if the student is unable to make choices and decisions.

Within a psychological curriculum in individualized reading, the student may choose how he/she wishes to be evaluated, covering the subject matter read. A variety of techniques may be utilized for the student to reveal knowledge and skills acquired. Sequence in evaluation with a psychological curriculum resides within the learner. Pertaining to stages that students go through in moral development, as an example of sequence, Kohlberg[5] emphasized the following based on his research:

I. Precoventional Level

At this level, the child is responsive to cultural rules and labels of good and bad, right or wrong, but interprets these labels either in terms of the physical or the hedonistic consequences of action (punishment, reward, exchange of favours) on in terms of the physical power of those who enunciate the rules and labels.

II. Conventional Level

At this level, maintaining the expectations of the individual's family, group, or nation is perceived as valuable in its own right, regardless of immediate and obvious consequences. The attitude is not only one of conformity to personal expectations and social order, both of loyalty to it, of actively maintaining, supporting, and justifying the order, and of identifying with the persons or group involved in it.

III. Post-conventional, Autonomous, or Principled Level

At this level, there is a clear effort to define moral values and principles that have validity and application apart from the authority of the groups or persons holding these principles and apart from the individual's own identification with these groups.

Objectives in the Curriculum

When viewing clearly stated objectives, the educators may well know what will be taught to students in the class setting. Excessively broad goals with diverse vague interpretations may have little value in teaching learning situations. Vague goals could include to develop the rational person, the good citizen, the democratic person, and the knowledgeable being. No direction is provided the classroom teacher, with such vague statements in determining what to teach, be it knowledge, skills, or attitudes.

When objectives are clearly stated, they need not be written in measurable terms, as behaviourists would desired. Clearly stated ends may be written as either general objectives and/or measurably stated objectives. Too frequently, educators believe that a good objective is definitely stated in measurable terms only and contains an indicator. After instruction, the teacher may then measure if a student has or has not attained a measurably stated objective. With general objectives, the teacher can also evaluate if a student is moving in the direction of goal attainment.

Measurably stated, also called behaviourally stated, objectives, are advocated in teaching-learning situations for a variety of reasons. Thus a teacher can be perfectly clear on what is to be taught when measurably stated objectives are emphasized in instruction. Guesswork is not involved in terms of *what* is to be taught. If an objective is truly stated in measurable terms, all viewers should be able to agree on which knowledge, skills, and attitudes will be taught.

If a teacher announces to students, prior to instruction, what they are to learn as a result of teaching, certainty is involved in the learner's mind as to what is to be achieved. The student then need not guess which facts, concepts, or generalizations are to be acquired.

Since the learning opportunities guide students in direct achievement of each measurably stated end, alignment of means to ends is then in evidence. After instruction, the teacher measures to ascertain if precise objectives have been attained by students. The test, if clearly written, should be valid in that the items therein relate directly to the measurable stated objectives. Alignment of tests to objectives is a must.

Lay people may wish to know how well students are achieving. Test results from each student can help to answer that question. Test result are in numerical terms so that parents and other interested adults can understand the achievement levels of students. Objective reporting of student achievement may then appear in the local newspaper, on radio, and on television. Comparisons may be made of last year's achievement of students as compared to the present school year. This can be done by comparing a student's progress from the previous to the present school year, Or, for example, last year's fourth grade might be compared with the fourth grade of the present school year. Comparisons have been made state by state of student achievement on the Scholastic Aptitude Test (SAT). Making these kinds of comparisons has been called the "wall chart" to notice differences in attainment.

State mandated and/or district wide instructional management systems (IMS) also advocate and implement the utilization of measurably stated objectives. Both approaches stress a basics curriculum. Thus a common set objectives is to be achieved by all students. No student may then select which objectives to achieve and which to omit. Common learnings (knowledge objectives) are available for all to attain. Slow learners may take more time to attain these objectives, as compared to average and talented learners. A core of objectives for all to attain does not discriminate among students as to some acquiring more sophisticated subject matter as compared to others, such as the slow learners. An essential body of knowledge has been selected which each and every student is to achieve.

General objectives were popular in teaching-learning situations during the 1970's and earlier. There still are educators who prefer the more ended objectives, or general objectives as compared to the more restricted, structured measurably stated objectives. General objectives, clearly stated and with no indicators, state in a broader way what will be taught, such as to develop within the student an understanding of consequences of World War II. The general objective with clarity states what a teacher will teach students and that being the aftermath or results of World War II having been fought.

General objectives provide a teacher with more flexibility in interpreting an end as compared to that which is measurably stated and contains an indicator.

Pertaining to a taxonomy of educational objectives, Brubaker[6] wrote:

> One of the main benefits that has resulted from recognition of the three domains is integrated teaching and learning. That is, curriculum planners have recognized the importance of integrating thinking, feeling, and acting in the learning process. Attention has been given to the important role of feelings and physical movement in a person's learning. Previously these two dimensions of learning were often neglected in the interest of low level cognitive processes such as memorizing and recalling information (facts).
>
> The levels or grades within each domain of the taxonomy can be useful to the curriculum planner. For example, the adaptation of the Bloom taxonomy shown in the table below can help the curriculum planner find the cognitive level of each question he asks. (You will note that higher levels of the taxonomy involve thinking processes at lower levels. For example, a Level 4 question involves thinking processes at Levels 1, 2, and 3.)

Bloom Taxonomy

Category Name total	*Description*	*Tally Column (per cent of Questions Asked)*
1. Memory	Student recalls or recognizes information.	
2. Translation	Student changes information into a different symbolic form or language.	
3. Interpretation	Student discovers relationships among facts, generalizations, definitions, values and skills.	
4. Application	Student solves a life problem that requires the identification of the issue and the selection and use of appropriate generalizations and skills.	
5. Analysis	Student solves a problem in the light of conscious knowledge of the parts and forms of thinking.	
6. Synthesis	Student solves a problem that requires original creative thinking.	
7. Evaluation	Student makes a judgement of good or bad, right or wrong, according to standards designated by students.	

The challenge to the curriculum planner is clear: The level of question asked should be relative to the questionnaires goals and objectives for asking the question. For example, if the curriculum planner as questioner needs specific information from a group, a memory question is appropriate. If "brainstroming" is used by the curriculum planner, higher level questions will elicit many and diverse answers for the group to consider.

Balance among Objectives

In designing the curriculum, adequate emphasis needs to be placed upon diverse kinds of objectives and goals, be they measurable or general. Teachers, supervisors, and administrators need to evaluate which type of end—knowledge, skills, or attitudes should receive major emphasis in teaching-learning situations.

There have been educators who largely stress students attain knowledge objectives. Thus learners are to attain an adequate number of vital facts, concepts, and generalizations. If higher cognitive objectives are emphasized, complex concepts and generalizations will be prized much more highly than factual content for student attainment. Skills objectives then need thorough implementation so that salient concepts and generalizations can be acquired. These skills include critical thinking, creative thinking, and problem solving. When thinking critically, students separate facts from opinions, accurate from inaccurate statements, and fantasy from reality. Separating into component parts such as analyzing subject matter is involved in critical thinking. Creative thinking stresses hypothesizing, originality, uniqueness of ideas, as well as divergent thinking. Fluency of ideas and flexibility become key concepts in guiding students to think creatively. Problem solving emphasizes students identifying a problem which involves a perplexing situation. Uncertainty exists in the mind of the learner as to which path to follow when thinking of answers to a problem. An adequate amount of subject matter needs to be gathered from different reference sources in answer to the question.

Then too, there are educators who stress the importance of students developing well in the affective or attitudinal dimension. To achieve well in terms of attitudes, students need to have learning activities which are highly interesting, possess much purpose, and provide adequately for each learner. To have interesting classroom experiences, learning activities which lack purpose of reason, as well as experience opportunities to learn which are too complex or excessively easy cannot assist students to attain well in the attitudinal development.

Students need to be heavily involved in choosing learning activities, from among alternatives. In this way each activity selected can be of interest, purpose, and provide for difference among students. Planning of activities by students with teacher guidance, not dictation, might well assist students to develop better attitudes.

A teacher determined curriculum consisting of objectives, learning activities, and appraisal procedures might not be of interest to students. Nor, do students perceive purpose or reason for learning under these situations, generally. Top frequently in a curriculum developed and implemented solely by the teacher, inadequate provision has been made for students of different achievement levels.

Selected educators may stress a balance among knowledge, skills, and attitudinal objectives. All three receive adequate emphasis. Perhaps, a balanced emphasis should be placed upon the three categories so that each receives adequate attention during teaching-learning situations.

Providing for Individual Differences

Each student differs from others in many ways. These differences include interests, abilities, purposes, and socio-economic levels. Students individually need to attain as much as possible. The classroom teacher needs to know and understand each learner well. As much information as possible should be secured about each student. The information should be utilized in a professional manner only, that being to do a better job of teaching. How might teachers provide for individual differences?

1. Experience cards listing possible activities to complete at each station should be written clearly. There are more activities at the diverse stations than any learner can complete. Activities are written on diverse levels of achievement. Those too difficult or too easy may be omitted by students. Each learner picks sequential activities that are on his/her achievement level. Individual differences might then be provided for. The student may select committee or individual endeavours to work on from the diverse stations.

2. An agreement may be signed by the student and the teacher pertaining to which activities the former should

complete. The student is largely responsible for determining the activities on the agreement form. Hopefully, each activity, be it committee or individual work, will assist students individually to attain optimally. The learner intrinsically needs to realize which tasks are too complex as well as too easy and should not be a part of the agreement. The purpose of the agreement is to guide each student to learn as much as possible.

3. With textbook use, a pretest can be written and given to students. From these test results, each student will be at a different place within the textbook. Thus for each learner, there is a starting point. He/she might then achieve sequentially form that starting point to provide for individual differences.

4. All students is a class may be taught together regardless of present achievement levels. No one then losses out on the more sophisticated knowledge. If tracking is stressed, the slow learner does not receive the same information as compared to the fast learner. Those who were formerly judged to the limited in achievement may progress with the others in the classroom, if the total class is taught as a unit. Mixed achievement levels, heterogeneously grouped, are then achieving and working together on diverse learning activities. Each student is adjusted to the curriculum, rather than adjusting the curriculum to the learner.

5. Homogeneous grouping may be used. Here, students are grouped according to their abilities so that homogeneity is involved. Thus, the top achievers are placed in one classroom, whereas the average achievers are placed in a separate room. Slow learners make for still another class of students in homogeneous grouping. In homogeneous grouping, the goal is to have students as uniform as possible in achievement within a classroom. The teacher may then have a better chance to provide for individual differences when the range of abilities within a classroom are lessened.

Pertaining to individual differences, Rubin[7] wrote:

> Intelligence can be defined as the ability to reason abstractly and to solve problems, but there seems to be no hard and fast way of measuring either intelligence or of predicting how well a child will do in school. There are, however, a number of factors that a teacher must recognize when concerned about the individual differences in children. One such factors is sex differences, particularly the differences between young boys and girls in growth and learning abilities. Another difference is in the home life of the child. In some homes more than one language is spoken, in others a dialect prevails. Also, the differences in the education of a student's parents, the socio-economic class of the family, the neighbourhood in which a student lives, and the composition of the family must be recognized as creating differences. Such factors should be taken into account if the teacher is to give each pupil the best possible education.
>
> Since research generalizations are often based on averages, we tend many times to talk of "average" children, but they don't really exist. It must be emphasized—and often—that because of many variables that make the student separate and unique, with his or her special assets, liabilities, and needs.

Unit Teaching

Selected teachers use unit teaching, especially in the curriculum areas of social studies and science. The name unit means oneness or a unity. The emphasis in unit teaching is for students to perceive relationship of subject matter. The classroom teacher assists students to relate knowledge and skills. Positive attitudes also need developing so that learners attain knowledge and skills objectives more effectively.

The development of resource and teaching units stress unit teaching philosophy. In addition to the objectives sections, unit plans tend to stress a threefold strategy in teaching. To start a unit, initiating activities need to be in evidence. These activities establish interest and purpose within the unit to motivate learners. After the initiating experiences, developmental activities need to be in the offing. With development experiences, students engage in depth learning of content, abilities, and the affective domain. Meaning and understanding of content acquired is vital. Culminating activities follow the developmental experiences. To culminate a unit means to end it satisfactorily. Culminating activities emphasis review, practice, and perhaps, some drill. Interest in the unit should remain high during the time given to the entire unit.

In each unit, a variety of learning activities needs to be in the offing. Reading as well as audio-visual materials should be utilized as learning opportunities for students. There are activities in a unit that are appropriate for each ability and achievement level of students.

Towards the opposite end of the unit teaching continuum is the textbook approach. A single or multiple series of textbooks used in sequential grade levels could provide the majority of objective students need to attain in terms of knowledge and skills. A few additional learning activities, such as selected audio-visual aids, could provide for variety of experiences and elaboration of subject matter contained in the basal text(s): Scope and sequence then basically reside within the textbook. The teacher needs to provide readiness, prior to students reading from these textbooks. Readiness experiences for students prior to reading silently might involve the teacher building background information directly related to what students will be reading, learners seeing the new words on the chalkboard and identifying each correctly, as well as being able to use words individually within sentences. Finally, prior to students engaging in reading, one or more purposes needed to be identified. Thus when students read silently, they will locate answers to these purposes or questions.

After the silent reading has been completed, a discussion may follow involving ideas gleaned.

Compared to unit teaching, basal textbook approaches of instruction are more structured and subject matter centered. Also, the abstract greatly overshadows concrete and semi-concrete experiences for students. Textbook approaches tend to be more formal and less open-ended and flexible. Objectives to be achieved focus largely upon a single reference source rather than a multi-media approach. Less provision for individual learning styles is in evidence since reading as largely the learning activity utilized.

However individual differences may be provided for by using a either unit teaching or the textbook(s) approach by adjusting each activity to individual differences among students.

Pertaining to the writing of daily lesson plans, Reisman and Payne[8] wrote:

> There are many formats for writing lesson plans. Some instructors require students to specify everything: prepare long-term and short-term goals, translate these into detailed list of objectives, set performance goals for each objective (pupil) must get 80 per cent of test items correct), describe procedures and materials to match each objective, schedule time for instruction, describe extended activities for reteaching, remediation, or enrichment, and set evaluation procedures. Objectives can become one-sentence paragraphs. To some extent, lesson plans in the detail required in pedagogy courses are not carried into the real world of teaching.

Grouping of Students for Instruction

Numerous means are available to group students in the classroom. Homogeneous grouping emphasizes placing a uniform set of learners in one classroom who have similar ability and achievement levels. Thus the gifted and talented would be taught in a separate room. The average achievers as well as slow learners would also be placed in separate classrooms for instructional purposes. Uniformity of achievement is then desired to teach a class of students. This cuts down on the range of achievement in a room as compared to mixed achievement levels of learners being in the same room. With less of a range in achievement, the teacher can do more large group instruction in homogeneously grouped students.

Heterogeneously grouped students make for a wide range of attainment within any classroom. The slow, average, and fast students are all taught in the same room. Within the heterogeneously grouped students in a classroom the teacher could divide students into small groups such as a fast, average, and lower achievement level for teaching purposes.

A different way of grouping learners for instruction would be the non-graded school. No grade levels exist here. Rather, students experience continuous progress. The gifted and talented are taught on a level where sequential progress is made with the sky being the limit. Average achievers too are taught where their starting point of academic achievement is, followed by optimal ordered progress. Slow learners would also achieve as rapidly as possible: however, their abilities would not permit the rapid progress made by the gifted/talented, as well as the average achievers.

Team teaching can be utilized with both homogeneous and heterogeneous grouping. A team approach emphasizes two or more classroom teachers planning the objectives, learning activities, and evaluation procedures, cooperatively, for teaching a given set of students. Teacher on a team should be given time during the school day to plan instruction. Thus, built in inservice education is in evidence. Teachers might then learn from each other during planning sessions. Secretaries and aids should do the routine work of a team of teachers so the latter can utilize their professional time more wisely for planning to teach students. One teacher of the team teaches in large group instruction. Whoever teaches in large group instruction, perhaps sixty to ninety students, may change off with other team members on a different day or days. After large group instruction, committee endeavours on the part of students is in evidence. Generally, five to eight students should be in each committee. All team members assist committees to clarify what was presented in the large group session. Additional activities and experiences also are pursued in these committees.

A third level of team teaching is individual study whereby each student with teacher guidance decides upon activities and experiences to pursue.

The philosophy of team teaching is quite different from the self-contained classroom whereby a single teacher plans for teaching students. The self-contained classroom teacher selects objectives, learning activities, and evaluation procedures in teaching a given at of students. There might well be no planning for instruction with other teachers. If the self-contained classroom teacher does minimal visiting with other teachers, opportunities here for inservice education diminish greatly.

A completely departmentalized plan of teaching usually is in evidence on the junior and senior high school levels. Each teacher plans for and teaches a specific academic area, such as history only, to a given set of students. The departmentalized teacher has completed a major in course work on the baccalaureate degree, or higher, in the academic area being taught on the junior or senior high school levels. Departmentalization can also be emphasized on the intermediate grade levels of the elementary school. Departmentalization emphasizes a teacher teaching in his-her academic area of speciality.

Class length will generally be forty-five to fifty minutes for each session of teaching a specific classroom of students. This is followed, in sequence, by teaching other classes of students in the academic area of speciality. Thus, a departmentalized teacher may teach, for example, five or six sections of students with twenty-five in each class, during each school day. It is more difficult then to get to know (six sections times twenty-five in each class) 150 students taught as compared to the twenty-five learners in the classroom for the self-contained teacher in the classroom. Teachers need to know and understand each student well to do the best job of teaching possible. Information pertaining to each student should be utilized to assist learners on an individual basis to attain more optimally. It is more difficult to relate subject matter areas in departmentalization as compared to the self-contained classroom. Time schedules can also be more rigid and formal for departmentalization, as compared to team teaching.

Magnet schools have as their ultimate goal the integration of students from diverse racial groups. A magnet school, as a model, has more teaching materials, better trained/educated teachers, and facilities, as compared to the regular public schools. Students together with their parents select, in large cities, whether or not the former is to attend a magnet school. Definite quotas exists in terms of numbers from each racial groups as to how many are accepted to attend a *magnet* school. *Magnet* school are considered a substitute to busing of minority students to achieve racial integration. As the name magnet indicates, students are to be attracted, as a magnet, to attend an educational institution. Thus the magnet school and its curriculum must be appealing to students and their parents.

Education by choice (EBC) was a concept salient in public schools during the 1970's. There are still selected school emphasizing EBC. With EBC, the student and parents chose a selected type of curriculum for the former. Thus, on the elementary level for intermediate grade levels, the following types of curriculum exists from which a choice could be made:

1. a basics curriculum which stresses the three R's (reading, writing, and arithmetic);
2. an activity centered curriculum whereby the different academic areas were learned within the framework of construction, art, excursions into the community, dramatization, and puppetry and marionette activities. Pupils were perceived to be active, not passive beings in teaching-learning situations;
3. non-graded schools whereby each pupil achieved as much as possible with no designated grade levels;
4. an integrated curriculum in which subject matter areas lost their boundaries and borders within the framework of problem solving activities.

Secondary students and their parents with education by choice could choose, from among the following alternatives:

1. the performing arts curriculum;
2. mathematics and computer science;
3. science, including physics and chemistry;
4. a foreign language curriculum.

Within each of the above named curricula, a general education emphasis would be in the offing.

The voucher system has been a rather recent approach in permitting parents and the student to select a school for the latter to attend. The student and parents may evaluate which school the learner is to attend. The school ultimately selected, of course, may bypass the local school. With student/parent selection, from among many alternatives, the best educational programme, hopefully, will be chosen.

The money available for schooling from public funds can be used to attend the school of the students choice. Transportation costs will generally be the responsibility of the parents. The voucher system can be compared with the market economy. In the market arena, individuals choose which products to buy. Popular products will survive on the market, whereas those goods and services not selling well will be eliminated due to buyers needs and demands. The same philosophy might then be applied to the public schools, those whose services are obtained through the voucher system will do well and expand. Where the demand for the services of a school are weak, the institution will either become better through inservice education or wither away. Either a weak school improves its teaching/educational services or it may no longer exist. With the market place philosophy, increased demand for a school's services of quality teaching increase the supply of those institutions deemed to possess excellence.

SUMMARY

Numerous designs of the curriculum have been discussed. These include:

1. separate subjects versus an integrated curriculum;
2. scope in the curriculum;
3. sequence in the curriculum;
4. measurably stated versus general objectives;
5. balance among knowledge, skills, and attitudinal objectives;
6. provision for individual abilities among students;
7. unit teaching procedures;
8. diverse means of grouping students for instruction.

Numerous philosophies were discussed pertaining to each of the above designs in developing the curriculum.

REFERENCES

1. Watkins, Beverly T. "An Education Professor Tries to Put His 'Fantasy School" Into Effect," *The Chronicle of Higher Education.* November 7, 1990, p. A3.

2. Shepherd, Gene D., and Ragan, William B. *Modern Elementary Curriculum*. Sixth edition. New York: Holt, Rinehart, and Winston, 1982, p. 83.

3. Ediger, Marlow, *The Elementary Curriculum*. Second edition. Kirksville, MO: Simpson Printing and Publishing Company, 1988, p. 94.

4. Phenix, Philip H., *Realms of Meaning*. New York: McGraw-Hill Book Company, 1964, pp. 279-280.

5. Hass, Glen, *Curriculum Planning: A New Approach*. Fourth edition. Boston: Allyn and Bacon, Inc., 1983, p. 166.

6. Brubaker, Dale L. *Curriculum Planning: The Dynamics of Theory and Practice*. Glenview, IL: Scott, Foresman and Company, 1982, pp. 28-29.

7. Rubin, Dorothy. *Teaching Elementary Language Arts*. Third edition. New York: Holt, Rinehart, and Winston, 1985, p. 22.

8. Reisman, Fredricka, and Payne, Beverly. *Elementary Education: A Basic Test*. Columbus, OH: Merrill Publishing Company, 1987, p. 9.

9

Learning Activities, Philosophy, and the Curriculum

Learning activities need to be selected so that students may achieve vital objectives. Each philosophical school of thought will emphasize specific criteria when activities are chosen.

Realism and Learning Activities

Realists advocate use of precise measurably stated objectives in teaching-learning situations. To achieve the objectives, learning activities need to be in the offing. Learning activities need to align with each objective. No more or no less content should be contained in the learning activity as is in evidence in any single objective. For example in the objective, "The student will explain orally how sedimentary rocks are formed," here, the learning activity should inherently contain content only on how sedimentary rocks are formed. No other content or subject matter should be in the learning activity. The learning activity becomes valid by being directly related to the measurably stated objective.

A variety of learning activities may be in the offing as long as alignment with the stated objective(s) is inherent. Thus excursions, video-tapes, video disks, films, filmstrips, slides, tapes, consultants, resource personnel, pictures, experiments, and demonstrations may be utilized as learning opportunities as long as subject matter is contained therein which assists students to achieve measurably stated objectives.

The curriculum areas of physics, chemistry, and mathematics provide models for the selection of learning activities. These academic disciplines provide specific subject matter which is verifiable. Truth here can be proven through the verification principle. The objectivity with which content in physics, chemistry, and mathematics can be made presents models for teaching the social sciences, the humanities, the fine arts, as well as physical education. For each curriculum area, predetermined measurably stated objectives are written prior to instruction. Teaching-learning situations stress students achieving the precisely stated objectives. Subject matter taught is objective, factual, and specific. What has been taught can be verified to demonstrate truth, accuracy, and objectives attainment. Scientific attitudes should be taught to students in all curriculum areas. The methods of science in teaching are a must to emphasize when learning activities are provided to students.

Along with demonstrations and experiments as methods of teaching, the teacher may also utilize programmed learning, be it in textbooks or software form. Programmed learning emphasizes the central role of the programmer in determining objectives, learning activities, and evaluation procedures. Thus, what is to be learned is broken down into small, sequential bits of information. A student, from the programmed textbook or on the monitor, reads a few sentences and views an illustration. The student responds to a multiple choice item to check comprehension pertaining to what was read. Response given to the multiple choice item is compared with the programmer's answer in book form or on the monitor. Feelings of reward accrue from responding correctly. If an incorrect answer was given, the student now knows the correct answer. Both, the student with the incorrect answer as well as the correct answer, are now ready for the next sequential programmed item. Thus read and view in illustration, respond, and check are sequences which are repeated again and again as the student progresses through a programme.

With behaviourism, students achieve precise ends. The precise ends provide direction for instruction or teaching-learning activities. Each step of acquired content is measured against the precise objectives of instruction.

Statistical procedures utilized in educational research emphasize realism, Wiersma[1] wrote:

> The term statistics has multiple meanings in educational research, but probably its simplest meaning is "bits of information." If one says that 632 students are enrolled in a specific school, this can be considered a statistic. The salary schedule and the numbers of teachers at each salary level for a district are sometimes called salary statistics;
>
> Statistics has a much broader meaning than simply bits of information, however. It also refers to the theory, procedures, and methodology by which data are summarized. It has been suggested that to some people, the terminology of statistics seems like a foreign language; although this may be true, the understanding and use of statistics is not so much a matter of identifying new terminology and symbols for already known concepts as it is a way of reasoning and drawing conclusions. Although the layperson often view statistics as an accumulation of facts, and figures, the researcher sees statistics as the methods used to describe data and make sense out of them.

Idealism and Learning Activities

Idealists emphasized in idea centered curriculum. Subject matter from diverse academic disciplines proud content for instruction. Content acquired assists students in mental development. Mind is real and needs stimulation. Subject matter needs to be challenging and vital. Worthwhile generalizations need to be achieved by students.

An academically inclined, concerned teacher needs to teach students to assist the latter to achieve important concepts, facts, and generalizations. From the imperfect to the increasingly more perfect person in development is the major goal of instruction. The teacher presents a model to students for emulation. He/she is enthused about the academic world and conveys these feelings and ideas to learners. The teacher needs to have much knowledge about students to guide them to achieve as much as possible in the academic domain. Teachers who implement idealism as a philosophy of education are proficient in awakening a desire within students for learning. Communication skills have been well developed by the teacher to impart an enjoyment for learning to students. The teacher reveals that he/ she is thoroughly engrossed in the subject matter taught. Each teacher is learning as preparation for the actual act of teaching is being pursued. Students need to grow and develop increasingly from the finite to the infinite or God.

Students need to engage in depth learning. Greater insights need to be developed in diverse academic disciplines. To develop self-intuition and personal responsibility for learning are worthy goals of education indeed. The teacher needs to stress questions which encourage thought, discussion, and analysis of ideas. Beyond the world of sense perception, the student realizes a metaphysical domain. Thus the student reaches out toward the Absolute. The Absolute represents the Infinite. Character development is highly important to an idealist in teaching students.

Learning activities for a curriculum of idealism will be represented by:

1. thought provoking discussions with in each academic discipline;
2. variety in methods utilized by the teacher to assist students to achieve significant meanings in subject matter presented;
3. the good, the true, and the beautiful which need emulating by students;
4. tasks which stimulate development of the intellect;
5. character development which moves in the direction of that which is eternal and Absolute.

Pertaining to Immanuel Kant and idealism, Eby[2] wrote:

> Kant accepted the existence of two entirely separate world orders, the physical and the ethical. Man exists in both. In one, mechanism rules and there is no freedom or intelligence. In the other the ethical universe, freedom and intelligence are found and these are essential for moral life.

In the moral universe or Kingdom, every individual is an end in himself and never a means for another's ends. Every man is an ethical, independent personality in whom the moral struggle of the universe is fought. Kant insisted upon the maxim: "Be a person and respect all others as persons." He exalted the individual and humanity and not the state or society. Moreover, he declared that "The only good thing in the world is a good will." In taking this position he made moral responsibility depend upon the motivation of the agent more than upon the results of the deed itself.

Experimentalism and Learning Activities

Experimentalism emphasizes a non-metaphysical world. The natural and social environment which can be experienced represents ultimate reality: Experience provides limits as to what can be known. The empirical world represents reality for human beings to experience. The supernatural and God cannot be known. Inadequate evidence is available to proclaim the existence of supernaturalism. The here and the now through experience present problems which need identification and solutions. Experimentalists believe there is no role for speculating about the hereafter and heaven.

The universe and what is therein is not static or changeless. Rather, open-endedness as a concepts is in evidence. The open-ended universe is shown through change, novelty, and the unknown. Human beings interact with the environment. As they do, learning occurs be it new ideas, language, inventions, and content. Modifications come about as new experiences continually accrue. The individual as well as the natural/social world change as a result of these interaction. One learns always in relationship others in society. The person is never as island unto the self.

Since individuals can know *experience* only, changes occur in one's knowledge, attitudes, and skills. One then attempts to get closer to knowing the real world as it truly is. However, it is not possible to know the real world as it truly is. Each person is limited to that which can be experienced. To test what is true, hypothesis are tried in life-like situations. Hypothesis are educated guesses based on the best knowledge available. Testing hypotheses are attempts to come as close to reality a possible through experience. There are no absolutes, according to experimentalists.

Values and morality are held to be tentative and subject to change. They are developed in society as individuals interact with society. Values and moral criteria are human needs. The public decides upon standards. Each standard is continually tested in society and may need modifications and changes. Society, not the individual, determines standards for values and morality. Experimentalists do not believe in analyzing a possible metaphysical domain. Metaphysics emphasizes that which exists beyond the use of the five senses. Experimentalists reject the idealist position of universal laws in values and morality. Rather, changing beliefs are in evidence. The changeless, the eternal, and the everlasting do not exist. What is conceived to be static, certain, and absolute merely represents tentative values and morality. Human beings are the measure of all things, according to experimentalists. As times and situations change so do values and moral standards. Situations change too within a certain time interval. One situation is different from another. This requires that values and moral standards be appropriate within a given situation.

Experimentalists emphasize the world of experience to students as learning activities. The following emphasize experimentalism as a philosophy of education:

1. avoiding dualisms in life such as moral standards versus living in society;
2. using intelligence to solve problems for all individuals, not the few only;
3. assisting students to be quality members of committees in school as well as in society;
4. becoming responsible persons to live in a democratic society;
5. solving identified life-like problems.

Evelyn Dewey[3], daughter of John Dewey, in 1919 wrote:

The development of a democracy demands that nothing be done to interfere with the fluidity of the populations: there must be no barriers built between different groups and occupations; everything must be kept as open as possible to promote free and sympathetic communication. This demands common interests among all the people; and the strongest common interest between people widely separated by space and occupation is the evolution of their government to the satisfaction of them all.

Existentialism and Learning Activities

Existentialists emphasize developing the authentic person who makes choices from among alternatives. To be human is to make decisions. If others make these decisions. This is a personal choice. Humaneness is then lacking if the person does not choose for himself/herself. Choices may be awesome and critically vital. Tension and anxiety may be involved in the making of choices and decisions. Each person is responsible for the consequence of selecting from among other possibilities.

Each person is an individual that basically lives a life of separation from others. Society attempts to have individuals conform to societal standards. The authentic self is lost in these situations. Death comes ultimately to all. At the same time, individuals need to find essence or purpose in life. The purposes are not given to any person but must be found. The individuals then must find purpose or reasons for life.

The human condition may emphasize isolation, aloneness, anxiety, and alienation. An authentic person makes a difference in life with choices and choosing in the decision making arena. The non-authentic person feels that nothing can be done to make for changes in society and in relating to others. The non-authentic person lacks the feelings of being human. There are no guidelines or absolutes in making choices. The world is open ended and humans can shape their very own individual destinies, according to existentialism.

Choices made are quite subjective and not based on something functional only or knowing the real world as it truly is. Rather, the individual attaches meaning to situations, events, deeds, acts, and occurrences. Subjective truth resides in the eye of the beholder. Doubt may be in evidence when decisions are made. Anguish may also be an end result of decision making. Truth is not forced upon the chooser by an Absolute being or

God. Nor is there an objective, empirical world which imprints itself upon the perceiver. Values then come from the individual. Each person needs to chart his/her objectives in life. He/she must be willing to stand alone and feel isolation, as a result of choices made. A human being needs to be entirely free to choose and to make decisions. Only then does a person become human, not an object.

Learning activities emphasizing existentialism as a philosophy of education might well include the following:

1. Values clarification whereby one encounters personal standards of morality and character;
2. Units on history, literature, philosophy, religion, art and music, in which the learner realizes subjectivity of content within the framework of values and decisions made by individuals;
3. Free choices of learning activities to emphasize decision making skills;
4. Choices made which reflect aloneness, awesomeness, and anxiety;
5. Authentic behaviour, not facades, emphasized in relating to others.

Pertaining to existentialism, Pulliam[4] wrote:

> Existentialism is not a functional philosophic system in the sense that educational goals or a statement of school theory can be derived from it. Existentialistic thought is highly individualistic and directs its attention to the self-fulfillment of each person. Stress on the unique experience of each individual and sensitivity to the problems of building personal values are found in the writings of existentialist philosophers. The work of Buber, Jaspers, Kierkaegaard, Heidegger, Marcel, Sartre, and Tillich are used by teachers interested in fostering spontaneity and authenticity. Educators who think of themselves as humanistic are often attracted by existentialism or its psychological counterpart, phenomenology. Existentialism raises questions about the assumption that education is primarily an agency of society for perpetuating cultural values or adjusting the child to a life-style accepted by the adult community.

Perennialism and Learning Factors

Perennialists emphasize universal truths. The universals go beyond the sensible world of the natural (science) and social (human made knowledge) world. Ultimate reality consists of time-tested truths which are beyond the objective, real world (realism) as well as the world of experience (experimentalism). Ultimate truths are not created by human beings, but are represented in the metaphysical realm. Metaphysics pertains to that which is beyond the sensible world. Truth, goodness, and beauty are represented objectively within the framework of the mataphysical domain. Through logic and reason, one can in part know objective reality contained in the Forms or heaven as emphasized by Plato. The Forms exist beyond the sensible world of experience. Perfection exists in the Forms or heaven. What exists in the sensible world are imperfect copies of that which is represented in the Forms.

The cultivation of the intellect emphasizes use of reason and logic. Intellectual tasks should predominate in the curriculum. The abstract is preferable and superior to the semi-concrete, as well as the concrete. The human mind needs to encounter learning activities which elevate thought.

Ideals such as the Forms are genuinely real and objective. The Forms exist independent of the observer. The forms emphasize universal truths. The Forms exist regardless of an individual's or person's perception. Thus the Good, the True, and the Beautiful are objective and exist independently of observations. The test of truth stresses one's ideas with what exists in the Forms. Metaphysical law stresses that the real is the ideal (The Forms) regardless of our position of reflection and observation. Through reason, the Forms, in part, can be known.

To live a good life is to move toward the perfect being. Lower values and beliefs consist of sense data, glory, power, love and self-realization. Higher values consist of the intellectual, the religious, the aesthetic, and the moral. Moral laws are based on natural law. Natural law is objective and universal. Quality thinking emphasizes reason and rational thought. Moral laws may be violated due to free will. Thus individuals may make wrong choices and violate the moral law.

Religious beliefs, as is true of the intellects, need to be cultivated. Facts, concepts and generalizations pertaining to religion need acquisition. The resultant religious beliefs need reflection, analyzation, and thought. Universal beliefs in religion need to be developed. Dogmatism and absolutes in religion are to be frowned upon. Raher, enjoyment and appreciation of richness in religious experiences need to be an end result.

Perennialism would emphasize the following learning activities:

1. Studying that which is good, true, and beautiful through the use of classical literature;
2. Emphasizing that quality facts, concepts, and generalizations endure and are not in a state of change;
3. Reading and learning from The Great Books of the Western World in their original or simplified versions;
4. Pursuing discussions stressing the cultivating of the intellect;
5. Advocating a liberal arts curriculum with emphasis placed upon the classics for content and style.

In his essay "The Conflict in Education," Hutchins[5] wrote:

> Nor is it possible for a person to have too much liberal education, because it is impossible to have too much understanding and judgement. But it is possible to undertake too much in the name of liberal education in youth. The object of liberal education in youth is not to teach the young all they will ever need to know. It is to give them the habits, ideas, and techniques that they need to continue to educate themselves. Thus the object of formal institutional liberal education in youth is to prepare the young to educate themselves throughout their lives;
>
> I would remind you of the impossibility of learning to understand and judge many of the most important things in youth. The judgement and understanding of practical affairs can amount to little in the absence of experience with practical affairs. Subject that cannot be understood without experience should not be taught to those who are without experience, it should be clear that these subjects can be taught only by way of introduction and that their value to he student depends on his continuing to study them as he acquires experience. The tragedy in America is that

economics, ethics, politics, history, and literature are studied in youth, and seldom studied again. Therefore the graduates of American universities seldom understand them.

Marxism and Learning Activities

Marl Marx (1818-1883) believed that individuals can achieve and accomplish within groups or the collective only. Individual endeavours do not make for needed changes in the economic and societal arenas. Marx saw worker oppression in his day by owners and managers of factories and places of business. The cards were stacked against workers due to laws, rules, and regulations having been established by the wealthy or the entrepreneurs. Religion and religious institutions also favoured the wealthy. Money for religious institutions and buildings came from wealthy persons. Churches advocated the free enterprise system of economics. Thus the prevailing system of government and religion needs to be overturned, according to Marx.

The triad of thesis (what is in evidence presently) consists of governmental and religious institutions favouring the wealthy whereas the antithesis (the opposite of the thesis) stresses the role of workers. Harmonizing the two opposites develops into a synthesis. The thesis, antithesis, and synthesis sequence continues until the workers eventually triumph over the entrepreneurs. Workers then control the means of production and distribution of goods.

Karl Marx based his philosophy on justice for workers in society. In the Old Testament, Amos, the prophet, was critical of the wealthy taking economic advantage over the widows and the fatherless. Numerous philosophers have compared Marx with Old Testament prophets calling for societal justice. Marx emphasized sharing goods in society. The early Christian Church is the book of Acts also stressed people voluntarily giving of what they had to a common treasury and receiving what was needed of live and endure. Each person contribute what was possible to the collective and received therefrom what was needed.

The Hutterite Mennonites in Montana, North Dakota, South Dakota, and Washington state also practice the collective concept, as presented in the Book of Acts. No individual owns an item, object, or property. All belongs to the commune. Each person on a Hutterite commune must work for the good of the collective, not the individual. The head of the Hutterite Mennonities is the minister. The minister is chosen by lot, not elected, to lead, guide, and direct the collective.

Below the minister is the business manager. The business manager transacts the selling of farm crops and livestock, among other items grown and produced, to the outside world. The business manager also buys farm machines and equipment for the commune. He must know prices to be able to operate at a profit for the commune. The business manager must also know how to deal with the buyers of Hutterite products, as well as sellers of goods and services to the commune. Next in line is the work supervisor who place adult commune members in different kinds of work. Diverse kinds of work need to be done by Hutterite men such as doing the field work for growing farm crops, tending to the laying hens in cage layers, taking care of cows, pigs, and butcher hogs, as well as providing for the needs of geese and turkeys.

Communal societies would emphasize the following in the curriculum:

1. students learning to work together for the welfare of the collective, not the individual *per se*. The individual can receive assistance and justice in a group setting only;
2. efforts of individuals being harmonized to make a cohesive whole;
3. cooperation rather than competition in school and societal endeavours;
4. emotional development which feels and believes that fulfillment on the collective is the ideal;
5. concern for individual members making for the welfare of the group.

Pertaining to Marxism, Meyer[6] wrote:

> The intellectual well springs which poured into the thinking of Marx, and especially into his 2,500 page *Das Kipital*, sprang from the philosophy of Hegel, from the Science of Darwin, and from the writings of the "utilitarian" economists. Marx had been

impressed by Hegel's ideas of state evolution and by Darwin's theory of biological evolution. To these he added his own philosophical idea of "must." Arguing that inasmuch as certain social and economic events had taken place in the past, Marx insisted that certain further developments must necessarily occur in the future. At the bottom this was something of a stimulus response formula applied to social and economic events, but growing out of historic and cultural antecedents. Since to Marx's mind these developments were altogether inevitable, the author of *Das Kapital* addresses himself to the task of giving us a blueprint of tomorrow's better society, and what is more important, to fashion the formula for attaining it.

SUMMARY

There are diverse learning activities which may well be provided for diverse philosophical schools of thought. These include:

1. a variety of activities, concrete to semi-concrete to abstract which assists students to achieve behaviourally stated objectives, as emphasized in realism as a philosophy of education. Alignment of activities with the precise objectives is a must;
2. subject centered, not activity centered, tasks to assist in mental development of learners, as advocated by idealism as a philosophy of education;
3. flexible steps of problem solving in which each problem is life-like and relevant in the societal arena, according to experimentalism as a philosophy of education;
4. decision-making, from among alternatives, by students in an existentialist curriculum;
5. a study of great ideas of the past, the classics, as stressed by perennialism;
6. collective endeavours for students in a Marxist centered curriculum.

REFERENCES

1. Wiersma, William *Research Methods on Education*. Fifth Edition. Boston: Allyn and Bacon. 1991 pp. 306-307.

2. Eby, Fredrick. *The Development of Modern Education*. Second Edition. Englewood Cliffs, N.J.: Prentice-Hall, Inc. 1964. p. 414.

3. Dewey, Evelyn. *New Schools for Old: The Regeneration of the Porter School*. New York: E.P. Dutton and Company. 1920. p. 336.

4. Pulliam, John D. *History of Education in America*, Fourth Edition. Columbus: Merrill Publishing Company. 1987. p. 177.

5. Noll, James Wm. and Kelly, Sam P. *Foundations of Education in America: An Anthology of Major Thoughts and Significant Actions*, New York: Harper and Row, Publishers. 1970. p. 355.

6. Meyer, A.E. *The Development of Education in the Twentieth Century*. Englewood Cliffs, N.J.: Prentice-Hall, Inc. 1962. p. 322.

10

Innovations in the Curriculum

Innovative ideas are needed to improve the curriculum. Public schools receive much criticism from the newsmedia, be it deserved or a scapegoat approach from shortcomings in society. Nevertheless, any profession must desire to improve their performance. Teaching is no exception. Better and improved objectives, learning opportunities, and evaluation procedures need to be in the offing for students.

Pertaining to John Goodlad's research results in his book *Teachers for Our Nation's Schools* (1990), Pauline Gough[1] wrote:

> Goodlad points to the low priority given to teacher education in schools and colleges of education in major universities, the paucity of rewards available to faculty members who devote themselves to preparing teachers, the weak or non-existent processes of professional socialization for students, the disjuncture between what happens on university campuses and what happens in collaborating schools, the lack of connection between theory and practice.

The Cry for Reform

Educational literature and writings call for reform. The lay public and newsmedia also call for reform. The concept *reform* in education has become a household word. Students are not learning to read, write, and compute. They are not prepared to enter the world of work after graduation from formal schooling.

Test scores of high school graduates is not going up on the ACT (American College Testing) tests. On the National Assessment of Educational Progress (NAEP), students are not improving in higher levels of thinking. And so, the criticisms continue. The following quote emphasizes the slogan of reform[2]:

> The pendulum metaphor is probably too tame for the intense difficulties public schools will face in the 1990's as reformers try to fashion a movement that addresses the unfinished agenda. At Charlottesville, President Bush, said, "the American people are ready for radical reforms." The next new years will tell how long that mood can be sustained. Meanwhile, school reformers have their work cut out for them.

Much subjectivity occurs when stressing which courses should go into the high school curriculum. The following are shown in contrasting ideas as to what should be inherent in the high school curriculum:

1. the liberal arts versus vocational education;
2. college preparation versus terminal education courses;
3. tracking of students versus students of diverse abilities learning from each other;
4. performance objectives to achieve in order to fraduate versus a certain number of credits (Carnegie units) based on time spent in different courses in the classroom;
5. meet minimal standards to graduate, as revealed by cutoff points on a state mandated test versus general faculty agreement, from grades received by a student, that a learner should receive a diploma to show high school graduation.

Since the above disagreements, among others, exist in terms of what makes for reform in education, consensus is not available to agree upon what makes for a quality curriculum for students.

No doubt, educators and others, continually talk about reform and rarely state in which direction the high school should move in terms of objectives for students to achieve.

During the 1970's and early 1980's considerable emphasis was placed upon a needs assessment programme. Surveys and interviews were then conducted within a school district to determine objectives for students to attain. If a questionnaire was utilized, objectives were listed and respondents were to rate each objective on a five point scale. Responses from parents were averaged separately from those of the students in school, as well as from teachers and administrators. It was difficult and time consuming to conduct a needs assessment in order to secure objectives, rated highly by respondents in the questionnaire for students to achieve. Then too, change is with us continually. Thus respondents may respond one way on the questionnaire and modify their thinking a few days later. Truth tended to be in the eyes of the beholder when responding to questionnaire items. A lack of consensus was certainly in evidence from needs assessments made in diverse school districts. Objectives from students to attain then lack clarity and general agreement.

Computers in the Classroom

Much criticism is given to the lack of computer use by teachers and students in the classroom. In society, computers are utilized in all walks of life, basically. Banks have provided computerized printouts of bank statements to customers as well as bank balance statements for instant withdrawal of cash using a plastic card. Supermarkets provide a computerized list of items purchased, as well as the price of each item at the checkout counter. These are just a few examples of the many uses of computers in the societal arena.

Software for different curriculum areas in the public schools increases at a rapid rate of publication. Types of software programmes include drill and practice, tutorial, diagnosis and remediation, simulation, and games. Many programmes have been tried out in pilot studies for sequential content, as well as appropriateness and relevance for different units of study. So often, computers are idle in the classroom. Numerous reasons are given for this situation:

1. one computer is not adequate for twenty-five to thirty students in a class;

2. a lack of software available, directly related to the current unit being taught;
3. software content is not on the understanding level of learners;
4. management problems occur when a computer is shared between classrooms;
5. a lack of time in a busy school day for computer use.

Advocates of heavy computer use in the classroom give the following reasons for their thinking:

1. it frees teacher time to work with small groups and individual students when computer service is utilized to teach the majority of learners in the class;
2. it represents what is current in technology which is highly useful in society and therefore utilitarian in the curriculum;
3. it provides for individual students since quality order of learnings occurs in the software;
4. it benefits students with self pacing of content covered on the monitor;
5. it assists in individual development as well as group or social development among students.

Philosophy of software and computer utilization emphasizes a technological approach to education. When securing objectives of instruction, computer use looks toward the future in terms of what will be. Other materials of instruction, such as reading and audio-visual aids may be used concurrently.

To be useful, software and computers will need to be:

1. increasingly user friendly so that ease of operation is in evidence;
2. more abundant in numbers so that each student may benefit optimally;
3. utilitarian in that inherent subject matter for students relates directly to the unit of instruction being taught;
4. orderly so that students experience sequential success;

5. controlled by the student, not vice versa, if it is to meet criteria of existentialists. Existentialists prize the individual to determine his/her own destiny. Thus, the student would need to make choices from among alternatives, if technology is to be utilized as learning opportunities or other media are to be used instead, in the curriculum.

Pertaining to change brought on by technology, Flake, McClintock, and Turner[3] wrote:

> Many careers are already in the process of change. Typewriters are being replaced by word processors. Professionals are finding themselves sitting in front of word processors and writing their own material instead of talking into dictaphones. Architects, engineers, and artists are working with computer-aided design systems. Librarians now retrieve information and conduct literature searches online. People on longer assume that everyone works 9 a.m. to 5 p.m. in an office; a number of people work at home and send information to the office via modem. Robots are assembling cars—and even computers.

Distance Learning and the Curriculum

Distance learning refers to a presenter being removed miles or kilometres from the local class in the school setting. The presenter could be quite far removed in distance from students in class. The dish antenna on the local school grounds picks up the singnals from the presenter, be it on a college/university campus. The dish antenna receives the signals and relays them to the monitor or receiver in the classroom. The monitor/receiver is just like a television screen. Content on the screen is observed by students within an ongoing unit of study.

Each distance learning presentation should have a completed manual which states that objectives to be achieved by students. By looking at the objectives, the teacher secures an overview of the telecast. Readiness activities provide background subject matter to students so that the telecast will be more meaningful. The background information developed by the teacher assists students to attend better to the ongoing presentation.

Content from distance learning may be used by students as information needed to solve problems, to achieve behaviourally stated objectives, or as general education in liberal arts curriculum. Students may also select, from among alternatives, to view distance learning presentations. The later sentence stresses existentialism as a philosophy of education.

Effort to learn from a distance learning presentation may be due to:

1. inherent interest in the presentation;
2. the will of the learner;
3. rewards (reinforcement) for doing well on a content validity test;
4. the human condition presented therein, such as absurdities in life, alienation, despair, dread, and loneliness (existential concepts).

Pertaining to guidelines for school innovation. Guskey[4] wrote:

> Broadening the scope of planning and implementation will not only encourage the integration of innovations but enhance opportunities for collegial sharing. When different strategies are implemented simultaneously, not everyone will be doing the same thing at the same time. Practitioners are likely to be at different stages of implementation. This can be an advantage: Experts in one strategy can serve as models, mentors, and coaches for beginners;
>
> The overarching reason to broaden our thinking about implementing new ideas, however, is that a broader view will promote synthesis of innovative strategies. Achieving optimal integration of innovations will not be easy, but is essential if school improvement efforts are to sustain momentum, continue to expand, and bring about the intended results. The primary task that lies ahead, therefore, is not so much finding individual ideas that work as making a collection of ideas work together.

Cooperative Learning in the Classroom

Cooperative learning stresses group rather than individual endeavours. A group of three to four students learn from each other in ongoing lessons. Sharing to ideas, not competition, becomes a major objective. Assisting others within a committee instead of each achieving at individual rates of speed is emphasized. Group dynamics becomes salient in that member is to be valued and accepted. The group should achieve as much or more, as compared to individualized or large group instruction.

Heterogeneous, not homogeneous, grouping is advocated in cooperative learning. Students can learn from each other, be they slow, average, or fast achievers. Learners in a group study and discuss challenging ideas. The slow learner is to be brought up to achievement with faster achievers. A levelling process is to occur in achievement among students of diverse ability and achievement levels.

Advantages given for cooperative learning are the following:

1. democracy is in evidence with equality of opportunity and subject matter acquisition being open to all;
2. students are not labelled in terms of being slow, average or fast learners. Each can contribute in a group to share knowledge, as well as to raise questions;
3. a common curriculum is available to all students in a committee, regardless of ability and socio-economic levels;
4. respect for all becomes a major goal in the curriculum;
5. each learner advances within a group, rather than as individuals. In society, persons individually also need to work harmoniously together with others.

Disadvantages which may be given for cooperative learning include the following:

1. the gifted and the talented may have to adjust their achievement to that of the slow learners;
2. individual initiative and endeavours may be hindered on the part of students;
3. interests, purposes, and styles of learning differ among students;

4. existentialist students may prefer a highly individualized approach to learning.

Pertaining to pragmatism (experimentalism), Organ[5] wrote the following on group versus individual endeavours:

> Those who defend the fourth view of man and the world believe no integration is adequate that does not take full account of the society in which man lives. School and society theory and practice, and present and future must not be places in polar opposition. "If I were asked to name the most needed of all reforms in the spirit of education," wrote Dewey years ago, "I should say: 'Cease conceiving of education as mere preparation for later life." Since we are thinking about American education, we are thinking of a democratic society. The principles of a democratic organization of society may be stated as the following:
>
> 1. Respect for the individual;
> 2. Equality of citizens;
> 3. As much liberty for each individual as is comparable with the general welfare;
> 4. Co-operation for the common good.

Pertaining to pragmatism (experimentlism), Organ[5] wrote the following on group versus individual endeavours:

> These principles act as a check and balance on each other. At some time quality needs to be stressed more than liberty; at other times liberty should be stressed. There arise occasions when individualism is more important than fraternity; and there are occasions when the interests of individuals are subordinate to the interests of the group. Democracy is no fixed organization of ideals; it has not permanent hierarchy of social values. The person who is trained to live in a democracy cannot be given a static education. A democratic education cannot be a procrustean education. Children should learn what is expected of them in a democracy through their shared experiences both within and without the schoolroom. Many of these experiences will be planned by an adult supervisor, for we cannot trust to luck that the right sort of experiences will happen to come to the child.

The Portfolio Idea in Evaluating Achievement

Diverse means of evaluation of student achievement is in the offing. Traditional norm referenced (standardized) achievement tests have been criticized for a lack of scope in appraising student progress. Too many facets of a student's achievement then are not being evaluated, such as achievement in oral communication and creative writing. Norm referenced tests contain multiple choice test items only.

Criterion referenced tests have been popular on the state and district wide level. The criterion referenced tests (CRT's) also contain multiple choice test items only. CRT's fail to measure facets of student progress and achievement. CRT's tend to emphasize fragmented learning in teaching situations. Thus with CRT's, measurably stated objectives are inherent. These objectives have been written on the state or district level. The classroom teacher selects learning opportunities so that goal achievement of students is possible. The number of objectives attained by each student is then measurable. Either a student has/has not achieved precise objectives.

The portfolio concept has been described as being more comprehensive for evaluations as compared to sole use of norm referenced and criterion referenced tests. With the portfolio, a broad collection of learner products may be incorporated therein, as well as test results. In the portfolio, a student could have cassette tapes of book reports and talks given, representative samples of written products, and art work, among other items. In the portfolio contents, the learner may reveal what has been accomplished and acquired.

Disadvantages given for portfolio use to reveal what each student has learned are the following:

1. subjectivity is involved in selecting representative items;
2. numerical results are not possible from learner products to report progress to parents, such as percentile ranks, standard deviations, and the semi-interquartile range;
3. educational philosophies are involved when determining how students should be appraised. Thus, objectivity is lacking in terms of how students should be appraised;
4. employers in the world of work and admissions counsellors at colleges/universities may have a difficult

time to appraise student learning using the portfolio idea.

Advantages given for utilizing portfolios. Instead of strict test results, to appraise student achievement are the following:

1. a broader spectrum of evaluation is in evidence, products and test results are available from each student;
2. students may be heavily involved in selecting products for the portfolio;
3. learners perceive increased purpose in evaluation when they personally are involved;
4. students may become motivated to achieve more since their products are involved in an open portfolio.

Team Leaders and the Curriculum

Team leaders, as a concept, are in charge of a set of teachers, generally two or three. The team leader is in charge of planning sessions with the other two or three teachers. Quality planning needs to be in evidence to select the best objectives, learning activities, and appraisal procedures. The results of planning, such as developing resource/teaching units and lesson plans, need to be implemented in teaching-learning situations to provide the best curriculum possible for students. Individual differences need to be provided for so that each student achieves as much as possible.

Built in inservice education is possible with the team leader approach. Thus team members may learn from each other in planning and teaching sessions. New ideas for teaching may be secured from planning sessions in terms of methods, procedures, activities, and experiences for students. When plans are implemented in teaching-learning situations, teachers observe each other teach resulting in new techniques, approaches, and ways of assisting learners to achieve continuous progress.

Advantages given for team leader approaches in teaching are the following:

1. comraderie can be developed among team members. Feelings of belonging are salient among teachers;

2. teachers can learn from each other in planning sessions devoted to lesson and unit instruction;
3. selected teachers feel more secure in a team situation as compared to being individuals in a self contained classroom;
4. professionals can observe each other teaching students and learn diverse methodology;
5. a team can generate and test more ideas in teaching-learning situations compared to the single teacher working by himself or herself in a self-contained classroom.

Disadvantages given for team leader approaches in teaching students include the following:

1. a motivated teacher may not wish to harmonize efforts within a team with less motivated teachers;
2. selected teachers may possess teaching styles emphasizing the individual rather than team endeavours;
3. students may not feel secure with a team leader approach in teaching, as compared to one teacher;
4. time to plan together may indeed be a problem for team endeavours;
5. friction and major disagreements might certainly be the lot of team endeavours.

Team leaders approaches in teaching may emphasize large group instruction, such as one teacher on a team teaching fifty students. Following the large group instruction, students are regrouped into committees. Each committee discusses what was presented in the large group session. Team members circulate among the different committees to offer guidance, direction, and extra materials of instruction.

Individual projects are also a part of the team leader philosophy of teaching. Each student selects a project which is perceived to be personally purposeful. Team members need skill to work with individual students in order to stimulate and motivate.

Pertaining to team approaches in teaching, McNeil[6] wrote:

> A team of teachers can accept responsibility for 100 students for a two-hour block of time each day. This allows the staff to assume different roles such as planning, lecturing, leading discussions, and counselling. A teacher in a team may be involved with a large class for a lecture, with a seminar-sized group of fifteen, or with students engaged in individual study. Teaching teams determine in advance the specific pupils they need to teach, the size of the groups, the length of teaching time, and the materials to use. Team leaders provide information for preparation of a master schedule for student guidance. Often, in a daily twenty-minute period, pupils, determine their own daily programme from the choices available on the master schedule;
>
> On branch of inter-disciplinary teaming is found in some middle schools in which four-person teams are composed of one specialist from among the areas of language arts, mathematics, social science, art, and science. Each specialist serves as the resource person for a subject area, doing much of the planning and teaching of that subject. Each teacher on the team, however, teaches all four of the academic subjects. The advantage of this arrangement is that correlation of the subject matter areas is easier and teachers are better able to attend individual students.

SUMMARY

Numerous innovations in education were discussed. Each innovation has selected assumptions. These innovations and their related assumptions are the following:

1. the cry for reform without stated direction or goals in learning;
2. computer use in the classroom with its philosophy of technology needing to replace much of what exists now in terms of materials and methodology of instruction;
3. distance learning with its emphasis upon bringing the remote into the classroom, such as videotapes developed removed from home base in its production and presentation. And yet through educational television, these programmes are being brought home to the local television monitor;
4. cooperative learning with heterogeneous grouping in which students in small groups learn from each other;

5. portfolios with a comprehensive approach in evaluating student progress. Additional products and data, other than test scores, are available to reveal student progress;
6. team leaders in which a set of teachers plan objectives, learning activities, and appraisal procedures for a class of students.

Innovations need to provide for students of all ability levels so each student may learn in much as possible. Tanner and Tanner[7] wrote:

> Finally, the curriculum must be in harmony with the nature of the learner and the ideals of a free society. At one extreme we have witnessed the educational failures of the romantic progressivists, who sought to turn the curriculum over to the "felt needs" and immediate interests of the immature learner. At the other extreme we have witnessed the educational failures of the traditionalists, who have conceived of mind as a vessel to be filled or as a muscle to be exercised through a reductionist drill-skill curriculum in the fundamentals. We have also witnessed the inequities that result when the direction of curriculum reform favours one group at the expense of another. Priorities in curriculum reform must be consistent with the widest public interest so as to serve all the people as optimally as possible.

REFERENCES

1. Gough, Pauline B., *Phi Delta Kappan* Nov. 1990 p. 179.
2. Greer, Peter R., "University Management of Schools: First Lessons," in *The Educational Digest*. Nov. 1990 p. 35.
3. Flake, Janice L., McClintock, C. Edwin, The Turner, Sandra. *Fundamentals of Computer Education*. Belmont, Cal.: Wadsworth, Inc., 1990, p. 298.
4. Guskey, Thomas R., "Guidelines for School Innovation" in *The Educational Digest*. Oct. 1990 p. 26.
5. Organ, Troy., "The Psychological Bases for Integration," *The Integration of Educational Experiences*. Chicago: The University of Chicago Press, 1958, pp. 39-40.
6. McNeil, John D., *Curriculum: A Comprehensive Introduction*. Fourth Edition. Glenview, Illinois: Scott, Foresman/Little, Brown Higher Education, 1990, pp. 201-202.
7. Tanner, Daniel and Tanner, Laurel. *History of the School Curriculum*. New York: Macmillan Publishing Company, 1990 p. 319.

11

Philosophical Deliberations and the Curriculum

Many decisions made in the curriculum of life are philosophical. Few choices are made empirically. Thus, in the school/class setting, teachers and supervisors need to choose from among the following which are quite opposite from each other:

1. programmed learning versus learning centers and open space education;
2. basal readers versus an individualized reading programme;
3. measurably stated objectives versus general goals in teaching learners;
4. teacher choice versus rather heavy learner input in determining objectives, learning activities, and evaluation procedures;
5. a textbook and workbook framework in teaching as compared to developing units of study utilizing a variety of media and materials.

It is quite obvious that empirical means can not be utilized solely in selecting objectives, learning activities, and evaluation procedures.

Experimentalism in Education

Experimentalists believe that one can only know what is experienced. One presently experience the here and the now. The human being cannot experience the hereafter. But, one reconstructs past learnings to harmonize with the present in the solving of problems.

Change is a key concept, according to experimentalists. Scenes and situations in society are not stable nor static. New inventions, technology, and ideas are continually with us. With change in society, new problems arise. Old solutions to the identified problems, in general, do not work. Thus, new data needs gathering in answer to the identified problem. After adequate data or information has been attained, a hypothesis or answer to the identified problem must be generated. The hypothesis is tested in life-like situations and revised, if necessary. Learners then need to develop skills in problem solving. Each person in the here and now has problems. These need to be identified and solved.

Experimentalists do not believe in absolute knowledge. Knowledge changes in terms of relevancy, accuracy, and usefulness. New knowledge is needed to offer solutions in problem solving situations. Formalism, rigidity, and dogmatism are three concepts which experimentalists reject in problem solving situations. Knowledge then is rather tentative, flexible, and subject to change. School and society do not reflect stability but change, openness, and newness. John Dewey[1] wrote the following:

> The nature of experience can be understood only by noting that it includes an active and a passive element peculiarly combined. On the active hand, experience is trying—a meaning which is made explicit in the connected term experiment. On the passive, it is undergoing. When we experience something we act upon it, we do something with it; then we suffer or undergo the consequences. We do something to the thing and then it does something to us in return: such as the peculiar combination. The connection of these two phases or experience measures the fruitfulness or value of the experience. Mere activity does not constitute experience. It is dispersive, centrifugal, dissipating. Experience as trying involves change, but change is meaningless

> transition unless it is consciously connected with the return wave of consequences which flow from it. When an activity is continued into the undergoing of consequences, when the change made by action is reflected back into a change made in us, the mere flux is loaded with significance. We learn something.

Experimentalists look at the consequences of an act rather than *a priori* statements or first principles. Thus, if a choice is to be made or a hypothesis to be tested, which consequences might accrue? There are no absolutes that one may cling to in the making of decisions. The ultimate decision made is open-ended. However, the end result should be that identified problems are solved. A change then results in moving away from what is to what should be. A believer in *a priori* statements believes that prior to any deed or act, universal ideas exist in leading one to make appropriate choices in school and in society. Opposite of *a priori* philosophies, the exeprimentalist looks at the consequences involved if one or several paths of action are followed as compared to other possible deeds or acts.

Experimentalists believe that the school be integrated and not separated from society. Too frequently, the school is an isolated institution from the larger societal arena. Rather, what is relevant and desirable in society must become inherent in the curriculum of the school. Pertaining to the school as a special environment, John Dewey[2] wrote:

> Hence a special mode of social intercourse is instituted, the school, to care for such matters.
>
> This mode of association has three functions sufficiently specific, as compared with ordinary associations of life, to be noted. First, a complex civilization is too complex to be assimilated piecemeal, in a gradual and graded way. The relationships of our present social life are so numerous and so interwoven that a child placed in the most favourable position could not readily share in many of the most important of them. Not sharing in them, their meaning would not be communicated to him, would not become a part of the forest. Business, politics, art, science, religion, would make all at once a clamour for attention; confusion would be the outcome. The first office of the social organ we call the school is to provide a simplified environment. It selects the features which are fairly fundamental and capable of being responded to by the young. Then it establishes a progressive order, using the factors

first acquired as means of gaining insight into what is more complicated.

In society, group action is involved in identifying and attempting to solve problems. In the school setting also, learners in committees need to select and solve relevant problems. A miniature society is then in evidence. Dualisms need to be avoided, such as separating school from society, or learner interest from effort. If learners perceive interest in learning, they will put fourth effort and reveal purposes in ongoing units of study. The learner must not be separated from the curriculum.

Morris and Pai[3] wrote the following pertaining to experience involving ultimate reality of experimentalism:

> Experience is the ultimate ground for human existence. If is both the originator and the supreme court of whatever we do or say. To put it bluntly once again, whatever reality it is what we say it is, and what we say it is founded in ordinary experience. Experience is as close as we can get to the "name" of reality. As exasperatingly non-substantive as this may be, it is the best we can do.
>
> Knowing, then, must take on a quite different notation in this philosophy, for we are immediately confronted by the necessity to settle for something much less than fixed and permanent truth as the end point of our epistemological labours. Since our reality is characterized by flux and movement and change, certainly our knowledge cannot be otherwise. We must therefore initially retrain ourselves to recognize that whatever knowledge is possible is temporary and tentative in character. If our conception of truth (knowledge) is ultimately "at the mercy of phenomena" as we experience them, as Dingle has said, then we must be willing to alter our truth and our knowledge as new and variable phenomena come into view.

A. Values, Ethics, and Experimentalism

Experimentalists definitely do not advocate absolutes in the values domain. Values change in time and place. They are applicable within a contextual situation. Values are tested in society and revised, if need be. The consequences of each value to be tested is significant. What might the end results be of each value to be tested? This is a highly significant question to answer on the part of experimentalists. Thus, there are consequences for each value tested within a larger geographical context. Values that have failed can be analyzed and evaluated. A new synthesis might then be in the offing. Values are developed and tested to improve the human situation, or move from the present to what should be. The "what should be" is open-ended and does not consist of closed, dogmatic ideals. Morris and Pai[4] write:

> But what, to ask the final question, ought we to want? To this the Experimentalist has no answer, for it is an ultimate question, and ultimate question have no answers. Since values are to be found in the context of experience, we will have to find out what we ought to want in the selfsame, relativistic circumstance of ordinary experiencing. There simply is no absolute answer.
>
> The only kind of sensible answer one can give is that people ought to want what they in fact do want when presented with all the alternatives and the knowledge of their consequences—which is no more than saying that a community of human beings employing a kind of public sharing of preferences and values and being intelligent about that whole business, can come to a working notion of the kind of civilization they would like to build, that is to say, the values that they would like to work for and attain. But in the working for and attaining of these values, other values have a tendency to suggest themselves. Humanity's valuing becomes, then, a constant creation of and accommodation to the changing moral environment about it. As the consequences that flow from humanity's principles change, the principles themselves change.

B. Aesthetics and Experimentalism

What is beautiful in the experiences of individuals in society? Why are selected music, art, drama, architecture, poetry, and other forms of literature relevant in comparison to other works involving aesthetics? There are no absolute standards in making judgements involving the aesthetic world, according to experimentalist. Each creative product and endeavour is tested in society. Individuals in society then accept, reject, or are neutral toward the endeavours of artists in diverse fields. Works of art then are tested in society. Artists notice the consequences of their products and processes. What is prized highly in a given place and time might not receive those ratings in other contextual situations, past and present. Gieger[5] writes the following involving change in society:

Nor can liberal education be simply content with efforts to preserve the past; it must take the lead in understanding, criticizing, and directing cultural change. The knowledge of the past contributes mightily to an understanding of the present is indubitable, and the past be cultivated for its own sake is something else again. It is present culture, not past, which is our problem. This does not signify that the more conservative view of liberal education is unconcerned with the present-day problems. But it would appear that the spector of discontinuity haunts the traditionalist here as elsewhere. Apparently he would prepare the adolescent by steeping him in historical materials of classic dimensions, and in the grand style, and then turn him loose, as an adult, on modern problems.

Realism in Education

Realists tend to believe that an objective real world exists, independent of any observer. The objective world can known as it truly is. Opinion and subjective judgements of persons is not important. Rather, through objective methods, the real world can be known through experimentation. Knowledge is held as being tentative until empirical evidence indicates hypotheses need changing. Rigid controls are necessary in scientific experiments in order that end results are truly objective. A learner needs ample experiences in science and mathematics since these curriculum areas emphasize objectivity and are highly relevant. Individuals live in a world of science. Each must respect natural law to life fully. Thus, principles of science in the curriculum should reflect the desire of learners to abide by the laws of nature. The laws are empirically based and not subject to the personal values and ideals of individuals. Content in science can be described in mathematical terms. Mathematics contains exact and precise subject matter independent of the feelings and beliefs possessed by any one individual.

In addition to science and mathematics being significant in the curriculum, other academic areas also contain objective content. Numerous studies have been made of words that learners need to master in reading. The identified words, gathered from carefully controlled studies, indicate those that have high utilitarian values and, if mastered, will cut down tremendously on reading errors among learners. Similar scientific studies have been made pertaining to words that pupils need to master in spelling. The identified words are useful for mastery learning. They consist of a core of words which all should learn to spell to minimize spelling errors on the part of learners. Other curriculum errors which contain objective subject material for pupil mastery include history (containing precise content on names, dates, places, and events) as well as geography. The latter has emphasized objective geographical phenomenon in time and place. The phenomenon include a study of rivers, valleys, plains, plateaus, oceans mountains, and seas, among others. Walquist[6] wrote:

> Realists generally agree in stressing the need of making philosophy scientific. A major part of the realistic programme of reform consists in emphasizing the close relations of philosophy to the sciences. There are those who think that the proper procedure for philosophy is to utilize the method of abstraction perfected in mathematics and made the basis of all scientific investigation. Generally, realists are agreed that the method of scientific analysis is the fundamental approach. The ultimate determinant of the truth of an idea is regarded as something beyond mere personal satisfaction, something external to the personality, and not dependent upon it. Consequently, truth must be discovered by objective means, as free as possible from the subjectivity of the experimenter. The realist is interested in the temperature of the room as registered by a gadget, not the impressions of the person in the room.

A. Values, Ethics, and Realism

Realists believe that values change. The change, however, is much more gradual, as compared to the thinking of experimentalists. Scientific methods need to be utilized by persons, individually and collectively, to ascertain that which has value. Opinions adhered to by individuals are subjective in content. Agreed upon adopted values need to be independent of personal feelings of involved human beings. Thus, objectivity is a key concept to emphasize in valuing according to realism as a philosophy of education. Human beings can discover and attain objective values. Agreement on these chosen values is possible.

Nature contains laws revealing what is right or wrong. Individuals can discover these laws of nature. To be successful in life, individuals must abide by the laws of nature. Morris and Pai[7] write the following pertaining to natural law:

> We may now speak of a nature-borne law of conduct that controls us quite as insistently and absolutely as does natural and ultimate truth. Natural law in ethical theory is usually called "moral law," and by this term we mean a law of right and wrong, that is embedded in the very structure of nature. Nature contains not just laws of gravity, thermodynamics, energy, and metabolism—that is, laws of the behaviour of completely material, subhuman entities; it contains laws of human behaviour as well.
>
> In speaking of group behaviour, we can cite economic and political laws, like the oft-cited Law of Supply and Demand of Lord Acton's famous law of political life: "Power corrupts, absolute power corrupts absolutely." Likewise in individual behaviour, says the Realist, there is a moral law intrinsic to the real, natural world that we must obey if we choose to be human beings. Injunctions against taking human life, laying, and cheating are the kinds of moral taboos that may go unwritten, even unspoken, in human societies; but they are nevertheless constantly operative in our lives, for they persist in time-space and exert their force on the conduct of all people in as imminent a way as the law of gravity. Furthermore, everyone knows these laws, whether we can utter them or not. We live "within" them if not always "by" them.

Morris and Pai[8] further write:

> Now, pure theory in epistemology is the analogue of natural or moral law in ethical discourse. Moral law is that law of behaviour which is beyond human utility, which is unconnected with our human interests or desires, and which consists merely in a statement of what the universe requires in the say of conduct. Moralists search for these laws for the same reasons scholars search for truth; just because they are laws of the cosmos we desire to know and hold them for their own sake. If they are seen to apply to this or that circumstance, so much the better; we make use of them. But the first and primary business of ethics is to know and commit oneself to natural and moral value.

Realists then believe there are moral laws independent of the observer's feelings and values. These laws must be discovered and observed. Objectivity and the methods of science are key concepts to emphasize in realism philosophy.

B. Aesthetics and Realism

What is beautiful? Nature has answers to this question. The answers are objective and do not involve human subjectivity. Personal biases should be omitted. The real environment contains beauty in nature. A beautiful bed of roses can be known as they truly are, independent of the observer. The roses do not need modifying and revising to emphasize beauty. They are beautiful in and of themselves.

Compositions in music also possess inherent beauty. Beauty in music is there, independent of observers and can be discovered. Observers therefore agree in time and space, as to what exemplifies beauty in music.

Feats in architecture need to adhere to natural law for a structure to remain endurable. Beauty inherently can reside within these structures. Independently of the observer, architectural endeavours either endure or do not endure. Nature has much to say in terms of which structures adhere to the laws of nature. Wahlquist[9] wrote:

> The realist is impressed with the objectivity of the external world. He holds that knowing is process of disclosure, not one of creation of the "reals." The real world is not subject to human whim and caprice. Experience is always experience-of, experience plus, reality. Furthermore, reality sets the limits upon experience in both form and content.
>
> The external cosmos is beyond the powers of man to know; the most he can hope for is to learn some of its secrets and to harness its forces. What he learns constitutes the great body of science. The only factual knowledge extant. One thing is sure; the world can go on without the aid of man; in some respects he is a fool to pass judgement upon it. In fact, if he would learn anything about the world, he must go about it objectively, eliminating selfish desires and personal preferences. The more he learns about this external world, in which he has his beginning and the forces of which constitute and control his being, the safer his future will become.
>
> In short, the realist tries to keep himself and his preferences out of the picture. In this respect, he feels that he clashes with both the idealist and the pragmatist. He desires to see things "Realistically," or as they actually are.

Existentialism in Education

Existentialists believe that one exists and then purposes need to be found or developed. The individual self then determines his/her own goals in life. There are no absolutes or exact guidelines in life to choose what is right or wrong. Each person must select and make decisions. To avoid making decisions is to lack being human. The choice then is to go along with the crowd. However, to be human involves making decisions and viewing the results of the choices.

The only broad criterion for existentialist to follow in choosing is to make moral decisions in a complete atmosphere of freedom. Others should definitely not decide one's destiny. One did not ask to be born and yet each person must make authentic decisions.

Moral decisions are difficult to make. An environment of awe exists in making authentic choices. Feelings of burden and responsibility are inherent in choosing from among alternatives.

Which objectives, learning activities, and evaluation procedures should be inherent in an existentialist curriculum? Existentialists believe in each person choosing objectives. In the school setting, the goals may be selected by learners with teacher guidance within the framework of an open-ended curriculum. A highly structured curriculum in which the teacher selects each objective for pupil attainment is definitely frowned upon by existentialists. Much teacher-pupil planning should, of course, be in the curriculum. Learners need to learn to choose and to make decisions, according to existentialists.

The teacher needs to emphasize ends, means, and evaluations procedures which stress the importance of pupils becoming increasingly responsible for personal freedom. The teacher should definitely not be a policeman. Rather, teachers realize their roles as providing for an open environment in order that the learner may select sequential experiences.

The teacher needs to encourage learners to study morality and moral standards in life. Each pupil must be encouraged to stand up for relevant purposes in life. The involved pupil needs to accept the philosophy that no person receives values, inherently, to accept. Rather, each chooses his/her own destiny and values in the curriculum of life. Purposes in learning needed to come from the learner, and nor from the teacher or others in society.

Learners should realize that significant decisions must be made in life which involve "fear and trembling." The everyday routine decisions made by any one person generally are not moral choices. Choices made which reflect ultimate changes in society in moving toward standards of morality are indeed relevant and goal oriented.

Pupils need to realize that important knowledge is subjective and not objective or science oriented. Each decisions made in life involves personal decisions in reaching a goal or goals. Thus, subjectivity in subject matter content is important. Literature, history, poetry, art music, drama, and architecture are indeed significant subjective curriculum areas. Each person can assist in shaping society in a moral direction when the humanities and the arts become an inherent part of the personal individual to make significant decisions.

Each person makes or breaks himself or herself. No other person or being is responsible for personal choices and decisions made. Each individual then must assume responsibility for consequences of decisions made. Blaming others for what happened in life is meaningless, according to existentialists. Each pupil needs to learn to accept responsibilities for thoughts, deeds, and actions.

Bowyer[10] wrote the following involving the thinking of Soren Kierkegaard (1813-1855), an existentialist:

> According to Kierkegaard, truth is not some prefabricated absolute that can be found outside the individual. Truth, he believed, can be attained only by an existing individual, for truth is subjectivity. A description of man's existential situation involves a distinction between man's present state—the way he is—and his potential state—the way he ought to be. There is a moment in the life of the individual from what he is essentially to his existential condition, from essence to existence.

Bowyer[11] further wrote:

> Kierkegaard's existentialism emphasizes individualism (not the group or crowd), subjectivity (not science or empirical means of

arriving at truth), introspection (looking within the personal self), and feeling (rather than objective facts). Kierkegaard emphasized freedom of the individual rather than logic, mechanism, or determinism.

Existentialism then emphasizes:

1. Individual rather then group endeavours. The individual exists and then chooses his/her own destiny;
2. Subjective ideas rather than the methods of science in making choices and decisions. The individual is the decision-maker;
3. Feelings rather than subject matter which can be tested and proven. The arts then need heavy emphasis in the curriculum. Individuals possess feelings. Decision-making is an awesome responsibility;
4. Each individual makes the self rather than living a predetermined life. The person chooses, makes choices, and decides. There is no predetermined life in which individuals merely do what was preordained prior to the lifespan of any one person.

A. Values, Ethics, and Existentialism

The existentialist looks of the self for values. The major criterion to use in the valuing domain is morality. Moral decisions are to be made in a completely free environment. Other beings must not dictate what is ethical or right. If the self looks toward others for ethical decisions, one no longer is human.

Existentialists believe that each person to be human, needs to select that which is ethical. Permitting others to choose for the personal self evades responsible behaviour. Each must choose what to do ethically within a contextual situation. Consequences for making choices rest with the chooser. Strumpf[12] writes the following pertaining to the thinking of Jean Paul Sartre, a leading existentialist:

> Man is always obliged to act in a situation, that is, in relation to other persons, and consequently his actions cannot, must not, be capricious, since he must take responsibility for all his actions. Moreover, to say that man must make his essence, invent his values, does not mean that one cannot judge human actions. It

is still possible to say that one's action was based either upon error or upon self-deception for any man who hides behind the excuse of his passions, or by espousing some doctrine of determinism deceives himself. To invent values, says Sartre, means only that there is no meaning or sense in life prior to acts of will. Life cannot be anything until it is lived, but each individual must make sense of it. The value of life is nothing else but the sense each person fashions into it.

The inner directed person making moral decision and accepting the consequences is important to existentialists. The existentialist does not blame others for outcomes of decisions made since the self made the choices. Choices made may not lead in the direction of making friends. In fact, alienation may occur as a result of speaking out and doing, in the morality domain. The existentialist may well be likened to one acting alone and by himself or herself.

What then is ethical to do? The individual must make this decision to be human. No one else can make this choice for the chooser. Self-gratification or focusing upon personal gains does not agree with criterion set forth by existentialists. Rather, what is moral needs emphasis in the decision-making arena.

B. Aesthetics and Existentialism

What represents beauty in the natural and social environment? The individual, alone, is responsible in choosing what is beautiful. Responsibilities in making the choices lie with the chooser, alone. Choices made may lead to unhappiness and feelings of loneliness. In making choices, the personal decisions are made in relationship to other human beings, never in a vacuum. Beauty is in the eye of the beholder. Universal standards cannot apply. Each person is unique and experiences life in its everyday tragedies, anxieties, and tensions. Art products need to reflect situations in life experienced by the individual.

Idealism and the Curriculum

Idealists believe in an idea centered curriculum. One cannot know the real world as it truly is, but the observer obtains ideas only pertaining to natural and social phenomenon. Universal ideas rather than specifics are significant, according to idealism, as a philosophy of education. The universal ideas remain rather stable in time and place, and are not subject to continuous change. Bigge[13] wrote:

> Since idealism posits a reality that is mental, learning is centered upon operations of minds. An educable human learner, as distinguished from an animal to be trained, is an actualized, self-active mind. "Pupils and teachers are more than vital mechanisms or behaving organisms; they are living spirits." Learning is a process of mental growth within which a self or personality expands in its development of selfhood, self-consciousness, and self-direction. It takes place through contemplation, imitation, and reasoning. In final analysis, then, learning is the upbuilding humanity in the image of divinity.
>
> Students as learners are more than responding organisms or social units. They are finite personalities growing into the likeness of an Infinite Ideal; should capable of genuine initiatives. Their responses are the active struggles of these initiatives germinating and growing into bloom. Thus, selves, personalities, or minds are central in gaining and organizing knowledge. Experience, for idealists, is the active functioning of these mentalistic selves.

Idealists believe that people individually and collectively are finite beings. Each individual is limited as to what can be achieved or attained. However, each person must move away from being finite to become increasingly like the Infinite.

In moving away from finiteness and in the direction of infiniteness, the person must experience an idea centered curriculum. Mind is real and mind then must be developed. Horne[14] wrote the following pertaining to mind being real:

> Mind is Real. (a) Education, as a human process with a meaning to spell concerning the truth, seizes upon mind as the final useful appendage to the organism in its upward evolution. That which nature by spontaneous variation, the struggle for existence, and the survival of the fit bestows as its last best gift to the organism, education seizes upon to improve, this raising evolution from the unconscious natural to the conscious mental plane. The highest type of selective agency of man,—education, lays hold upon the highest selected product of nature,—mind, for further improvement, reality. Education by its emphases practices the saying of Sir William Hamilton, viz., "In the world there is nothing great but man; in man there is nothing great but mind." The school and also the other more general educative agencies of civilization lay all their stress upon mind as the most valuable,

> the most useful, the most real, element in life. Chosen last as the result of an incalculably long, prehistoric process of natural selection, mind has become first. Education may be pardoned for its ontological boldness if it questions reflectively whether the reality its selects as ultimate is not the ultimate reality. Is not reality mental?

There are selected curriculum area which idealists believe are relevant in guiding pupils in the direction of the Infinite mind. Universal ideals need to be acquired by learners in an idea centered curriculum. Providing needed subject matter include the academic areas of

1. reading literature, history, and geography;
2. writing including grammar, spelling, punctuation, capitalization, among other skills, needed to present clearly communicated ideas;
3. mathematics and science;
4. Other curriculum areas, such as health, art, music, and physical education.

Academic areas which assist in developing the mind and superior to other curriculum areas. However, to develop universal ideas, a learner needs to be perceived holistically–intellectually, morally, emotionally, socially, and physically. Human beings need to move beyond the observable to truly understand natural and social phenomena. Theodore Greene[15] wrote the following:

> My first presupposition, or basic assumption, is that man finds himself in a complex environment which he can in some measure know and to which he can more or less successfully adapt himself. This assumption falls halfway between radical skepticism, on the one hand, and all forms of absolutism or authoritarianism on the other. I believe that man can know something, but not everything; that he can know many things with increasing clarity and assurance, but that he can never, because he is incorrigibly finite, know anything with complete certainty and finality.

A. Values, Ethics, and Idealism

The idealist educator emphasizes universal values and ethics be developed by learners. Universal criteria are enduring in time and place. Secular and sacred literature in diverse historical periods of time as well as in numerous geographical regions have emphasized a universal ethic in the Golden Rule. "Do unto others as you would have them do to you" represents a universal standard of conduct.

Idealists advocate that experience of the senses is superficial compared to depth searching in terms of what is valuable. To understand and use the Golden Rule is complex. Understanding the universal ethic and how it operates in diverse situations is not easy. It is even more difficult to develop needed skills in utilizing the Golden Rule in every day experiences in life. Theodore Greene[16] writes the following involving liberalism in ethics pertaining to idealism, as a philosophy of education:

> Liberalism, so conceived, has its own basic values which it must defend at all costs because they condition its vitality and, indeed, its very existence. The specific virtues which it must espouse and the vices which it must combat can usefully be defined in the context of a liberal educational policy. The three basic liberal virtures are (a) serious concern, (b) intellectual and moral integrity, and (c) profound humility; the three corresponding vices are frivolous or cynical indifference, lack of integrity, and arrogance. Teachers should be hired only if they possess these three virtues, in addition to intellectual competence, and they should be fired either for incompetence or for exemplifying any one or more of these three vices. It should also be the prime concern of the school assiduously to foster these virtues and combat these vices in its students as well as to cultivate whatever intellectual and creative talents they may possess.

B. Aesthetics and Idealism

What makes for beauty in art, music, architecture, and literature, among other creative endeavours of human being? Human beings are limited or finite. The finite needs to continually move in the direction of the infinite. What exists in the natural and social environment needs improving in moving away from the limited to the unlimited. The creative artist then attempts to present universal content in artistic endeavours. Products in art reveal beauty in terms of ideals stressed. Ideas pertaining in the natural/social environment need to express artistically that which is enduring and universal. Going beyond what the senses portray is significant. Human beings need to search for beauty. Troy Organ[17] writes the following:

> Values are intrinsic to the world. The world supports and sustains men as they attempt to increase the values in the universe. The intuitive insights of the artist and the prophet give more accurate glimpses of the real nature of the world than do the hypotheses and the experiments of scientists. Since the view of the world as spiritual is held by those who believe the world to be ideal–like but do not believe in God, as well as by the supernaturalists, the term "idealism" is used to identify this position, even though the word is extremely ambiguous. Among its many uses it denotes both those who believe the world in mind-dependent, that is, reality is always and necessarily the object of a perceiving mind (subjective idealism) and those who believe the world is spiritual rather than physical and does not depend upon being perceived (objective idealism).

SUMMARY

Philosophy of education has much to say in terms of implementing objectives, learning activities, and evaluation, procedures in the curriculum.

The experimentalist educator believes that learners need to identify and solve relevant problems in a changing society.

Realists advocate using methods of science to obtain precise information involving the real world as it truly is.

Existentialists emphasize the importance of the individual making subjective moral commitments within an irrational world.

Idealists believe that universal standards and generalizations need discovering in moving from the finite to the Infinite Being.

Educators need to be students of philosophy. Diverse philosophical strands provide guidance in developing the curriculum.

Ozman and Craver[18] wrote:

> A study of philosophy of education seems imperative today, for we are in a critical era of transition. There has always been change, but seldom at our present accelerated rate, creating in

many individuals what Alvin Toffler has called the sickness of "future shock." In such an age, it is easy for people either to embrace more and more change with little thought to eventual consequences or to resist change and keep old values no matter what. Educational philosophers, regardless of the particular theory they embrace, suggest that the solutions to our problems can best be achieved through critical and reflective thought.

In one basic sense, we can say that philosophy of education is the application of philosophical ideas to educational problems. We can also say with equal force that the practice of education leads to a refinement of philosophical ideas. From this viewpoint, educational philosophy is not only a way of looking at ideas but also of learning how to use them is the best way. No intelligent philosophy of education is involved when educators do things simply because they were done in the past. A philosophy of education becomes significant at they point where educators recognize the need to think clearly about what they are doing and to see what they are doing in the larger context of individual and social development.

REFERENCES

1. Dewey, John. *Democracy and Education*, as quoted in *Selected Readings in the Philosophy of Education*, 3rd Edition, Joe Park, Editor, New York: The Macmillan Company, 1968, p. 87.
2. Dewey, John. *Democracy and Education*, as quoted in *Selected Readings in the Philosophy of Education*, 3rd Edition, Joe Park, Editor, New York: The Macmillan Company, 1968, p. 87.
3. Van Cleve, Morris and Young, Pai, *Philosophy and the American School*. Boston: Houghton-Mifflin Company, 1976, pp. 145-146.
4. Van Cleve, Morris and Young, Pai. *Philosophy and the American School*. Boston: Houghton-Mifflin Company, 1976, pp. 145-146.
5. George Geiger, "An Experimentalist Approach to Education" (Chapter 5), *Modern Philosophies and Education*. Chicago: National Society for the Study of Education—University of Chicago Press, 1955, p. 152.
6. Wahlquist, John T. *The Philosophy of American Education*. New York; The Ronald Press Co., 1942, p. 56.
7. Van Cleve, Morris and Young, Pai, *Philosophy and the American School*. Boston: Houghton-Mifflin Company, 1976, pp. 238-239.
8. Van Cleve, Morris and Young, Pai, *Philosophy and the American School*. Boston: Houghton-Mifflin Company, 1976, p. 239.

9. Wahlquist, John T. *The Philosophy of American Education*. New York: The Ronald Press Co., 1942, p. 365-366.

10. Bowyer, Carlton H., *Philosophical Perspectives for Education*, Glenview, IL; Scott, Foresman and Company, 1970, p. 241.

11. Bowyer, Carlton H., *Philosophical Perspectives for Education*. Glenview, IL; Scott, Foresman and Company, 1970, p. 240.

12. Strumpf, Samuel Enoch, *Socrates to Sartre*, New York: McGraw-Hill Book Co., 1966, p. 470.

13. Bigge., Morris L. *Educational Philosophies for Teachers*. Columbus: Charles E. Merrill Publishing Company, 1982, p. 31.

14. Horne, Herman H. *The Philosophy of Education*. New York: The Macmillan Company, 1927, pp. 257-285. (as quoted in *Selected Readings in the Philosophy of Education*. Third Edition: Joe Park (Editor), New York: The Macmillan Company, 1968; p. 146.

15. National Society for the Study of Education, *Modern Philosophies of Education*. Chicago: University of Chicago Press, 1955, p. 99.

16. National Society for the Study of Education, *Modern Philosophies of Education*. Chicago: University of Chicago Press, 1955, pp. 111-112.

17. National Society for the Study of Education, *The Integration of Educational Experiences*. Chicago: University of Chicago Press, 1958, p. 31.

18. Ozmon and Craver. *Philosophical Foundations of Education*, Fourth edition. Columbus, OH: Merrill Publishing Co., 1990.

Index

Outcome based curricule, 100-02
Ozmon, Howard, 1, 91, 206